ROUSSEAU

JEAN-JACQUES ROUSSEAU was born in 1712, in the city and republic of Geneva, to a family of French origin descended from Protestant refugees expelled from France. He died in 1778, at Ermenonville, near Paris, after a wandering life darkened by persecutions because of his independent and powerful writings, and troubled by ills both of body and mind. Influenced by the Bible, Plutarch, Robinson Crusoe, the great Latin classics, and the French moralists, Montaigne, La Bruyère, and penetrated by a passionate feeling for nature, his genius as a deeply religious and Republican thinker, and his great art as a writer of the pre-Romantic school assured him first place, beside Voltaire, among the writers of the 18th Century. His influence was immense on the generations which made the French Revolution, and it prolonged itself over the entire century following.

ROUSSEAU

M
ROUSSEAU

THE LIVING THOUGHTS OF

ROUSSEAU

PRESENTED BY

ROMAIN ROLLAND

WINNER OF THE GRAND PRIX OF THE ACADÉMIE FRANÇAISE, 1913

WINNER OF THE NOBEL PRIZE FOR LITERATURE, 1916

THE LIVING THOUGHTS LIBRARY

EDITED BY ALFRED O. MENDEL

1939

LONGMANS, GREEN AND CO.

NEW YORK · TORONTO

The Living Thoughts Library
is being published in Argentina (Spanish), Bulgaria, Canada, Czechoslovakia, Denmark, Finland, France, Great Britain, Holland, Hungary, Norway, Poland, Rumania, Sweden, the United States of America, Yugoslavia

Translation of the Introductory Essay by Julie Kernan

The Selections from *The Social Contract, Discourse on the Origin of Inequality,* and *Emile* are from the translations by G. D. H. Cole and Barbara Foxley from Everyman's Library. The remaining selections are from contemporary English translations now in the British Museum.

The woodcut portrait of Rousseau was made by Professor Hans A. Mueller

ROUSSEAU

FIRST EDITION

PRINTED IN THE UNITED STATES OF AMERICA

Life travels upward in spirals. He who takes pains to search the shadows of the past below us, then, can better judge the tiny arc up which he climbs, more surely guess the dim curves of the future above him.

PRESENTING

JEAN-JACQUES ROUSSEAU

Jean-Jacques Rousseau is one of the most striking examples of the power of a mind over its epoch. He penetrated, transformed and revolutionized the society of his century and of the century which followed. The rancour of the old crumbling world was not misplaced. It laid at his door, as at that of Voltaire, responsibility for all the upheavals of the 19th century: "It is Voltaire's fault! It is the fault of Rousseau!" was the mocking song of Victor Hugo's Gavroche in *Les Misérables.*

But between Voltaire and Rousseau, it was the second who played by far the most important part. Voltaire was the most brilliant star of a large and compact constellation: the Encyclopedists. Rousseau lived alone, and he fought alone. As we shall see, in his combats he even ran foul the hatred of the Encyclopedists whose morals he refuted and whose social ideas he surpassed. Voltaire and his great lieutenants, Diderot, D'Alembert, D'Holbach, Helvetius, personified above all the negative side of the new spirit, bent upon the destruction of the old society, its prejudices and its abuses; they were the critical and scoffing champions of free reason. Rousseau alone represented the constructive side, the affirmation of the new faith; he was the proclaimer of the Republic. The French Revolution claimed him as its originator; his apotheosis took place at the height of the Convention. It was Robespierre who decreed the transfer of his ashes to the Pantheon.

And yet it is certain that this was not the posthumous triumph of which Rousseau himself would have dreamed. There is every reason to believe that, like Voltaire, he would have denied the Revolution which acclaimed him. But great works always surpass their author. The spirit freed by them unleashes storms which cannot be foreseen. The social upheavals thus wrought are none the less their work. In spite of his protests against the rôle allotted to him by fate, Rousseau, the solitary, remains in history the great Precursor of the storm, the initiator of the new era.

The most extraordinary fact about Rousseau is that not only did he not foresee the consequences of his fame and genius, but that both of these came to him despite himself.

The life and work of Jean-Jacques Rousseau offer in literary history the case, perhaps unique, of a man of genius, upon whom genius descended not only unsolicited, but against his will.

He was born a little bourgeois of Geneva, timid, without will power, characterless, early delivered to all the risks of an adventurous life, dreamy, loafing, well enough endowed, but indolent, fickle, lazy, forgetful, at the mercy of every wind, with no spirit of application, no care of the morrow, and aspiring to nothing but the tranquillity of a mediocre and indolent existence – without any great needs beyond a sensual taste for romantic and erotic musings. Until his thirty-seventh year, nothing appears to have disturbed him. But suddenly, without warning, he was infused with genius, and like St. Paul, he was struck down by a thunderbolt of which I will speak ; he was illuminated, and the pen – that fiery weapon – was placed in his hand. He found himself thrown into the arena where the most illustrious champions of the human spirit were in combat before the eyes of an assembled world. And from the first stroke, he surpassed them all. With surprise and not without fear, he heard his own voice which he scarcely recognized, filling the amphitheatre with accents as powerful as those from a tribune of antiquity, attacking the most respected idols and shaking society to its very foundations.

He might well be terrified and swear that he would write no more. He was caught in the torrent which he himself had unleashed. He was the Republican who rose like an oak-tree, high above the existing monarchical order. And this passionate being always retained an inflexible, an unbelievable lucidity. He, who to that time had been a vagabond and dreamer, a sentimental and weakly anarchist, made of himself the most enlightened and firm of lawmakers.

All these powers within himself outdistanced him, and he aspired to rid himself of them. It is as though a formidable and temporary gift were bestowed upon him, an order from on high imposing a mission upon him and raising him above himself for twelve exalted years, twelve years of genius – after which he sank back again into the life of vegetation and dreaming for which he had always longed. But unbalanced by the enormity of the effort he had been called upon to make, and by the stormy repercussions of his flaming words, he fell into a sort of tragic delirium in which his sorrow was lulled by the beauty of his song.

He was born, on June 28, 1712, in that amazing "*town and republic of Geneva,*" home of the reformed evangelical religion, whose very existence was a paradox, surrounded and penetrated as it was by the great monarchical and Catholic States.

Jean-Jacques was proud of his origin, and all his life remained deeply marked by it. He signed himself : "*Jean-Jacques Rousseau, citizen of Geneva,*" and he claimed his rights as the "*citizen of a free State and member of the sovereign people.*" He dedicated "*to the Republic of Geneva*" his *Discours sur l'origine de l'inégalité.* Jealously he watched over the defense of "*his fatherland,*" despite the ingratitude it showed toward him and the persecutions of which he was the object. He never faltered in his praise of that city of working people and its republican customs. He always expressed for it a passionate love and sorrow at living away from it. "*Jean-Jacques, love your country!*" his father said to him when he was a child. "*You are a Genevan ; one day you shall see other peoples ; never will you see the like of your own.*" He never forgot this advice. "*Each time that he studied the question of government, he was always happy to find in his investigations new reasons to love that of his own country.*" In his criticism of all governments, "*he set apart one alone and proposed it as an example.*" It was that of Geneva.

He made no less staunch profession of Protestantism, although circumstances had led him in his youth to be converted to Catholicism. But in 1754 he solemnly re-entered the reformed Protestant church, in the full effulgence of his dawning glory, and he was bold enough to proclaim : "*I am a confessor of the Protestant faith in Paris.*" And whatever were the storms that he raised among the pastors of Geneva and Neuchâtel by his broad interpretation of Christianity, his tolerance and humanity, he attested that he had always "*followed as nearly as he could the doctrine of the Gospel. . . I have loved it, I have adopted it, spread and interpreted it, I am attached to it with all the zeal of my heart. All my writings are imbued with the same love for the Gospel and the same veneration for Jesus Christ. Nothing can be compared to the Gospel. This book must be preserved as the rule of the Master, and my books only as the commentaries of a pupil.*" At the time of his greatest triumphs in Paris, among the aristocracy of the court and the Encyclopedist philosophers, the enemies of God, he usually read the Bible in the evening ; and he read it over from one end to the other five or six times successively in the seclusion of his long nights of sleeplessness. He called himself, with some exaggeration, "*the only man in France who believes in God.*"

The Republic and God – this twofold love, this twofold faith – he had sucked at the breast of Geneva ; and it was this that had gone into his blood. It was this which distinguished him in Paris from all the French writers of his time.

Nevertheless, we should add that even in proudly maintaining his Genevan independence, he always showed a preference for France. He tried in vain to stifle this ; he admitted that he had always felt such a partiality for France that "*his heart beat with joy at its slightest success, and its reverses afflicted him as though they had befallen himself.*"

His family was, moreover, of French origin. He was a descendant of Protestant refugees expelled from France. His mother, beautiful and intelligent, Suzanne Bernard, died in giving him birth. On the paternal side, his forebears had been artisan watchmakers, robust and intelligent. His father, Isaac Rousseau, was kind but careless, violent, restless, a vagabond and adventurer, an inveterate reader. He inculcated this taste in his son and transmitted to him his roving disposition. The father and child, who was then six or seven years old, would surfeit themselves with the reading of novels, often passing the whole night in this way. "*Sometimes the father, hearing in the morning the sound of the awakening swallows, would say shamefacedly : 'Let us go to bed ; I am more of a child than you. . .'* "

But Jean-Jacques' best teacher, his Mentor, who went with him from the cradle to the grave, was Plutarch. "*When I was six, Plutarch fell into my hands ; I knew him by heart. I had read every novel ; they had made me shed torrents of tears before the age when the heart is interested in novels. From this there was formed in me a taste for the heroic and romantic which has increased since, and which ended by disgusting me with everything except that which fitted in with my fantasies.*"

The motherless child, abandoned by his father at the age of ten, ill fitted to life, found refuge from life in his dreams. A precocious *ennui du monde*, which is the precursor of romanticism, caused him to seek solitude in nature. He "*found himself more able to deal with the fanciful beings with which he surrounded himself, than with those he saw in the world.*" This "*society entirely supported by his imagination*" almost made him lose his way in life, and to cause the dissolution of his will power. It is well that during his childhood and the opening of his adolescent life, he had to do with good people. The memories of those years, in the first books of his *Confessions*, have a charming grace and abandon. Anyone who is not familiar with them, does not know the real Jean-Jacques. Usually he is only seen in the conventional picture created by his great books – argumentative, rhetorical, moralizing. It is to do him an injustice. His was a cheerful nature – loving, fascinating, light, volatile, forgetful, quick to follow every enthusiasm, incapable of resisting his inclinations, extremely weak and knowing it, but fundamentally sane, without malice or impurity. It is remarkable to note the incredible physical innocence which he kept in his wandering youth, without any guide to watch over him. His path led across the most dubious places, even vicious and polluted, without this cygnet tarnishing even one of his plumes.

He attracted people strangely, but he also disappointed them, by the unimaginable waywardness, giddiness, lack of consideration, lack of judgment, lack of memory, complete forgetfulness, with which he let fall tomorrow persons and things with whom he had seemed most taken today. He followed nothing up, interrupted everything that he began. Where was he educated ? At the age of twenty he knew nothing. Those who examined him, even the best disposed, came to the conclusion that he had no future, that the best he could do would be to become a little country *curé*. None of this worried him in the least.

The meeting with a woman decided his life. In 1728 at Annecy, he saw Madame de Warens, and he was smitten. Fifty years later in the last pages that came from his pen, he cries out with the same grateful love to his good "*maman*" : for the motherless child always sought maternity in love ; and in Madame de Warens he found this.

After brief attempts to live away from her, in obedience to the young *maman*, who wished him to find a career for himself – but without any desire to succeed – the little vagabond who had traveled on foot the roads between Annecy and Turin, over the Alps, then to Lyons, to Lausanne and Neuchâtel, and from there, always on foot, always dreaming, always loitering, to Paris – again returned to his *maman* who had now removed to Chambéry. And she, at last discouraged but charmed, took her young lover into her home. She was, like himself, tender and sensual, careless and visionary, kind, easy to excess, but strangely indifferent even to those who most loved her, forgetting them as soon as they left her ; she never knew what she had meant to Jean-Jacques ; or, if she did know, she did not care. But those three years – the three delightful summers that they lived together in the cheerful house at Charmettes near Chambéry (1738–1740) – were for Jean-Jacques a dream of Paradise. At the same time that he tasted "*happiness pure and complete*," he pursued his literary education – vagabond like his early life and in keeping with what his character always was – reading, without any plan, Montaigne, La Bruyère, Bayle, Bossuet, Voltaire. It was the latter – his future enemy – whose *Lettres philosophiques*, by Rousseau's own admission, "*most attracted him to study,*" and first stimulated him to write. "*The taste,*" he says, "*which I formed for this reading inspired me with a desire to learn to write elegantly and to try to imitate the beautiful coloring of the author who so delighted me.*"

Nevertheless, in summing up, one may say that his education always remained incomplete and most inferior to that of the great Encyclopedists : he did not have any great knowledge of the classics with the exception of Plutarch, Tacitus, Seneca, a little of Plato and perhaps Virgil. But he was sufficiently a genius to divine by intuition and to bring to life what he imbibed in the quotations used by great readers like Montaigne or Bossuet, and in his Swiss countryman Muralt for English literature.

Besides his greatest teacher was not any book. His master was nature. He loved her passionately from his childhood ; and this passion is not expressed in his writings by cumbrous descriptions ; nature imbued his whole being, she expressed herself by certain sober and arresting traits. She plunged him into ecstasies which were accentuated in his later days and which made him strangely akin to the great mystics of the Orient.

In 1741, bitterly deceived by Madame de Warens, his place beside her usurped during his absence from their nest, he expatriated himself and went to Paris. He was thirty years old, and his only resources were fifteen silver louis, the manuscript of a little comedy, and a new system of musical notation from which he expected fame and fortune. He always considered himself more of a musician than a writer ; and even after his first successes with the pen, he persisted – humorously – in his infatuation with the spirit of music, although he was never more than a passable harmonist, with little invention and even less training.

He began by losing his time and his money, loafing in cafés and in salons. But this was not useless to him; it was in this way he came to know Fontanelle, Marivaux, Condillac, and especially Diderot, who became his friend. He was also well liked by the ladies, who procured for this young Genevan vagabond, without qualifications – by a chance which was really scandalous (it was not surprising in those times!) – the post of secretary to the French embassy in Venice (May 1743). Having quarreled with the ambassador, he quitted this place in 1744. In Paris he refound Diderot and the support of the pompous *fermiers-généraux* (landed businessmen); he presented on the stage some little musical plays and adaptations of Voltaire and Rameau. He went to live (1754) * with a young hotel maid, Thérèse Le Vasseur, who remained his companion until death parted them. He was later to have several children by her; alas, all deposited by him one after the other at the foundling home. He gave himself all sorts of unworthy reasons for the act, reasons which never really satisfied him and which left him to the end pursued by regret and remorse.

At thirty-seven, he still found himself among the crowd of aimless scribblers who gathered up crumbs from the table of the Midases of finance and their consorts; and there was nothing to indicate his destiny, when in the summer of 1749, he was felled by the thunderbolt of which I have spoken. Of this

* After twenty-five years of living together, he ended by marrying her.

experience he could never speak without trembling.

He went one day to see Diderot, imprisoned for an infringement of the press laws in the dungeon of Vincennes. The heat was excessive. He had two leagues to go on foot, along an unshaded road. As he walked along, and in order to moderate his steps, he turned the leaves of an issue of a literary review. His glance fell upon an announcement by the Academy of Dijon offering a prize for the best discussion of the following question: "*Has the progress of science and art contributed to the corruption or to the improvement of morals?*" He was suddenly "*pierced by a thousand rays of light; a multitude of living ideas*" assailed him; he was suffocated, inebriated; he fell beneath a tree near the avenue, and here he passed a half hour in a delirium of thought, from which he emerged with the front of his jacket soaked with tears. "*At that instant,*" he wrote, "*I lived in another world, and I became another man.*" It was not only the answer to the question of the Academy which came to him, but in its train, as if the sluice-gates were opened, a torrent of "*great truths*" which would form the basic matter of his entire future work. The shock had revealed to him his true being.

He was exceptionally placed to perceive the social unease which was brewing at this period. He did not belong to the French and Parisian circles, to the rule of absolute monarchy, tempered by a loosening of morals and an ironic attitude toward life, in which the most independent writers, the Encyclopedists, managed to adapt themselves, profiting by the very abuses which they combated. He had passed his first thirty years in a happy and sleepy atmosphere as a little Swiss tramp, which life had made him into a truant school-boy, regardless of social restraints and laws. He was thus all the more sensitive to the moral and almost physical repression of the artificial world of letters and court-life in Paris. At first frightened and stifled, he had repressed his feelings of suffering, revolt and disgust. But these feelings were accumulating. And now they had exploded ! With one stroke, he uncovered the social evil – the corruption and iniquity of society. And the tremendous response to his first cry revealed a mission hitherto unsuspected by him.

For his success had surpassed by far not only his own expectations, but the rather mediocre value which he himself – rightly – attributed to his first work. Far more, public opinion seizing upon it, gave it a revolutionary meaning which Rousseau denied stubbornly but without success. In him was seen the destroyer of a civilization who claimed that all its conquests amounted to naught. His only claim was to save himself, and with him his little country of Geneva, by removing them from the contagion of that hypercultivated world, civilized to morbid excess and to the "deterioration of the species" – but without hoping for or attempting the cure of the incurable.

But man proposes, and genius disposes. Once the pen was in his hand, he could not bring himself to stop, and he had to go on to the end. His flow of ideas, increased by the unprecedented triumph of his first "*Discours*," threw him into "*a fermentation of heroism and virtue*," of which "*the seed had been planted in his childhood by his father, his country and Plutarch.*"

We should note that his "illumination" of 1749 coincided with the irruption of the bladder disease which was thenceforward to torture and intoxicate him until his death. His case seemed hopeless. In 1749 the doctors gave him not more than six months to live. We can imagine into what a frenzy this conviction would throw a sincere and courageous soul! Rousseau no longer had anything to withhold.

He withheld nothing. He saw only "*error and folly in the teachings*" of those philosophers he had previously treated with respect and who considered him as their ally. He saw "*only oppression and misery in the social order.*" And he said this without attenuation. He considered that "*to be listened to, he should make his conduct in accordance with his principles.*" And he did so. He changed his costume, renouncing white stockings and fine shirts, he sold his watch, discarded his sword, and clothed himself in a commonplace suit of thick cloth, and a round wig; he gave up his position as cashier and claimed to earn his living as a laborer, a copyist of music. It was a revolution which took place within him, as it did a century later in Tolstoi, who was inspired by Rousseau's example and lessons – "*I was really transformed.*" Nobody recognized him; he was no longer the embarrassed, shamefaced little foreigner, frightened by everything. "*Audacious, proud, intrepid, full of scorn for the morals, maxims and prejudices of his century, insensible to the scorn of those who had such prejudices, he crushed their little witticisms with his sentences as if he had crushed,* he said, *an insect between his fingers. What a change! All Paris repeated the acrid and biting sarcasms of this man who two years before and ten years afterward, could never find what he had to say nor words in which to say it. . ."*

If later on he said that he was persecuted, it was in this period of war, declared and waged by him without quarter on all the society of his time, that one must seek the source of the implacable bitterness which he aroused.

The Discourse on the evils of science, art and civilization was followed in 1753 by the *Discours sur l'origine de l'inégalité parmi les hommes*, whose social significance and revolutionary bitterness went far beyond the first discourse. Rousseau found himself carried away by the spirit of revolt burning within him and by the implacable logic of his thought, to denounce the idea of Property, which gives rise to inequality, the necessity for the regulation of this inequality by the State, and the fatal deterioration of States wherein power is arbitrarily usurped by rich men who end by reducing the human race to slavery. He denounced the plutocratic democracy of the future.* Many philosophers of the 18th century had already touched on these daring ideas ; but none of them had applied the slightest will power to giving active form to their speculations. Rousseau did nothing by halves. For him thought was not a game. He was terribly serious. Fear was aroused when he hurled his anathema against the rich, and again when he declared revolt a "*juridical action*" when it strangled or dethroned the tyrant

* "*In a monarchy the opulence of a private individual never places him above a prince ; but in a republic it could easily place him above the law. Then a government has power no longer, and the rich are always the real sovereigns.*" (Letter to D'Alembert.)

of "*despotism which was gradually raising its hideous head.*"

Added to the danger of such ideas, was the fact that by his genius as an orator he disposed of a tremendous means of influencing the masses. He created for himself an out-of-door style, forged to excite the masses, and wiping out every other style used by the desk-bound writers of the day.*

This can be seen in his third letter (to D'Alembert) *Sur les Spectacles* (1758) – 283 pages – a torrent of passionate eloquence which highly inflamed public opinion. Parts of it were already a Revolutionary speech. D'Alembert, intimidated – he, the illustrious savant, member of five or six learned societies – was fearful in crossing swords with this hitherto unknown man who had no other title than that of "*citizen of Geneva.*"

"*It would be very dangerous to struggle against such a pen as yours. . . You know how to please the masses, by the very scorn which you show for them. . .*"

And he compared him to Luther!

Rousseau wished for nothing so much as to bid farewell to the public and to the world, to leave Paris and retire into nature, alone. And he did this. He availed himself of an invitation extended to him by the wife of a *fermier-général*, the sprightly Madame

* "*It was no longer a question of speaking to the few, but to the (general) public. . . A change of style became necessary; to make myself better understood by all the world, I said fewer things in more words.*" (Preface of a Letter to D'Alembert.)

And his enemy, D'Alembert, agreed:

"*It is within your rights to be fulsome, yet read nevertheless.*"

d'Epinay, to come and live in a "Hermitage" in the forest of Montmorency. Here he took up his abode, April 9, 1756. "*It was only on that day*," he said, "*that I began to live.*"

His erstwhile friends, his colleagues, could understand nothing of this. They accused him of acting only to make people talk, or by inveterate misanthropy ; and Rousseau thought it necessary to explain himself in his letters to Malesherbes (1762). The real cause of his retirement, he said, was "*that unconquerable spirit of liberty, which nothing could overcome, and before which honors, fortune and even reputation were as nothing.*" He added with sincerity that "*this spirit of liberty sprang in him, moreover, less from pride than from indolence ; but this indolence is incredible ; everything terrifies him ; the slightest duties of civil life are insupportable ; a word to say, a letter to write, a visit to be made, when these are necessary, are a torture for me. . .*" All his youthful efforts to arrive, had but one object : "*retirement and repose.*" From the moment he could enjoy these, he hastened to avail himself of them. . .

His own demon was the cause of their destruction.

Alone at last in his "Hermitage," and savoring with great satisfaction what his sons, the German romanticists, were to call "*Sehnsucht*," "*Wonne der Wehmut*," "*the happiness of tears*," etc. – the erotic melancholy which he described in admirable pages, of feeling himself "*in the decline of life*" (he was 44 years old !) – and "*overcome by the need of loving which he had never been able to satisfy*," he abandoned himself to his erotic dreams.

"*It was June beneath the shady groves, there was the song of the nightingale, the babbling of the brook. . .*" He surrounded himself "*with a seraglio of houris.*" He called himself "*The extravagant Shepherd*" of this band. Soon his dreams took shape ; there appeared to him the heroines of his immortal romance – *La nouvelle Héloïse* – blond Julie and brown-haired Claire. He wandered with them in the forest of Montmorency. To make himself master of his dreams, he began by writing, without any plan, several scanty letters, the first two parts of the book. He was immersed in this work when a passion for Madame d'Houdetot, Madame d'Epinay's sister-in-law, set him on fire (the spring of 1757). But in those hours when he again assumed control of his work, he blushed, he was ashamed of perpetrating by his *Julie* so flagrant a denial of all his fine sermons against the world and the literature of love. "*After the severe principles which he had proclaimed with such vigor, after so many biting invectives against effeminate books, inspired by love and indolence,*" he gave himself over to the enemy. He tried in vain to free himself ; he was completely subjugated. He tried to redeem himself by "*turning his erotic reveries to a moral end,*" and in this he succeeded to the point that it is not possible to dispute the high morality of his works. This mixture of free passion and of sermonizing morality which today appears to us to make his romance weighty and stiff, added in his day to its indescribable success. Well could writers of his day attack him from jealousy – Voltaire descended to the lowest outrages – but public opinion was intoxicated, and above all, the ladies of the court. *Julie* caused the shedding of torrents of tears. All criticism was swept aside by a great wave of enthusiasm.

Nevertheless, Rousseau's tranquillity was troubled, and storms, partly sentimental, caused him to leave his Thebaid. He quarreled with his hostess, Madame d'Epinay, and moved into another house in the forest of Montmorency, at Montlouis, then to Montmorency itself where members of the highest nobility – the duke and duchess of Luxembourg – offered him the most delicate hospitality.

Again a fine target for the envious slanders of the literary men, who did not fail to deride bitterly this hermit, this man of nature, this scorner of society, who always managed to find lodging with the masters of finance or members of the court! Rousseau himself suffered from these contradictions; but he could not refrain from accepting, with affectionate gratitude, the benefactions which his noble friends offered him with such generosity. During the four or five years which he passed under their wing, he wrote his greatest works: *La nouvelle Héloïse* was finished there, the *Lettre à D'Alembert sur les Spectacles*, the *Contrat social*, and *Emile*.

He had planned that this was to be the end of his literary career. He had estimated that *Emile* and the *Contrat* would net him a capital of eight to ten thousand francs with which he would purchase a life annuity for himself and his Thérèse. After which he would go and live in the retirement of the provinces, writing at his leisure the memoirs of his life. He wished to make of this life "*a work unique for its unparalleled veracity, in order that at least once a man might be seen as he is within.*" These *Confessions* were not to be published in his lifetime, and were to be written like a monologue, filling a happy solitude, apart from all worldly tumult.

He suspected nothing of the frightful storm which was gathering over him, a storm that was to uproot him from his shelter in Montmorency and pursue him until the end of his life.

He had made numerous enemies: La Pompadour, the king's favorite; the formidable Premier and Minister, Choiseul; the moulders of opinion in Paris, Madame du Deffand and Mademoiselle de Lespinasse; the "philosophers" who saw in him a renegade from their secret society, and at their head Voltaire, full of jealousy and malice; the middle-class people of the law, the parliamentarians who began to suspect the danger latent within the audacious and revolutionary ideas of this foreigner; finally, that strange coalition of atheists and bigots who, irresolute up to that time, were now swarming about a book whose danger Rousseau himself did not suspect.

This book was not, as one might think today, the *Contrat social* which thirty years later was to become Robespierre's breviary, and which at that time passed relatively unnoticed,* but the most beautiful, the purest and most benevolent book he ever wrote, the gospel of toleration and charitable belief, free from all the prejudices of the churches – *La profession de foi du vicaire savoyard*, which formed the fourth part of *Emile*. This work was to seal the alliance against Rousseau of what he called the "*fanaticism of*

* At least in France, for it was burned in Geneva. And Rousseau had every reason to be indignant. "*My book,*" he said, "*attacks all governments and is not proscribed under any of them. It praises one government only and proposes it as an example; it is under this one that it is burned. The magistrate of Geneva punishes its own citizen for preferring the laws of his own country to those of any other!*" (Lettres de la Montagne, L. vi.)

atheists" and "*fanaticism of the bigots.*" Passions mounted to a paroxysm, and there were symptoms of a furious civil war. The publication of the *Encyclopédie* had kindled the flame. The two parties unleashed, Christians and philosophers, tore each other to pieces "*like mad wolves.*" "*Perhaps there was only lacking on both sides,*" wrote Rousseau, "*capable and trustworthy leaders for it to degenerate into a civil war, and God knows what a civil and religious war would have led to, when the most cruel intolerance prevailed on both sides.*" Rousseau, who suffered from this poisonous atmosphere, had wished by his *Nouvelle Héloïse*, his *Emile*, and his *Profession de foi* to bring peace to the two opposing camps, and to preach tolerance to them – he only turned them all against himself.

It took him a long time to realize his danger. He, usually so ready to harbor groundless fears, refused to understand the many warnings of his friends, alarmed by the approaching publication of *Emile.* Rousseau was bathed in the ecstasy in which he had written this book which replaced for him the sons he had had and lost. In the charming little château presented him by the Luxembourgs, surrounded by water like an "Isola Bella," for company his Thérèse, his cat and his dog, he did not hear the thunder on the edge of the forest of Montmorency. When he began to take fright, he fell from his heights and lost his head, seeing danger everywhere it was not, and accusing the Jesuits who had other things to think of at that moment, for they were being persecuted and expelled from all the Catholic countries. Physicians who have studied Rousseau's case, date from the end of the year 1761, the first grave crisis in his persecution mania. It was provoked by this unexpected blow, and was accompanied by a violent attack of his urinary disease, the torture of which led him for a moment to think of suicide.

It was in this state that there fell upon him the terrible decree of the Parliament of Paris. Less than twenty days after *Emile* had appeared in Holland, and before there had been time to distribute it in France, without preliminary warning, the Parliament condemned the book to be burned, and the author to arrest (June 9, 1762). On June 11, the book was mutilated and publicly burned at the foot of the great stairway of the Palais de Justice in Paris; and it was said openly that it was not enough to burn the book, that the author should be burned too. Rousseau's protectors, the highest nobility of France – the Luxembourgs, the Boufflers, and the Conti – were themselves fearful of being compromised with him, and urged him to flee. This he did, not without regret, on June 11. A fine passage in his *Confessions* recalls, with moving details, the night of his leave-taking and flight. He succeeded in reaching Swiss soil and, prostrating himself, kissed "*the land of liberty*" with great emotion.

He was not long in being disillusioned on the score of Swiss "liberty." His enemies pursued him with unbelievable relentlessness. Nine days later than Paris, Geneva in its turn burned *Emile*. Berne followed, then Neuchâtel. "*Throughout all Europe, a cry of malediction was raised against me, a fury of which the equal has never been seen. I was an infidel, an atheist, a madman, a ferocious beast, a wolf.*" He believed that the world had gone crazy.

It is scarcely surprising that a weak and soft-hearted man, unarmed, the prey of a torturing and poisoning disease, should have lost the balance of reason under the avalanche of hate which engulfed him, and that thenceforth he was to become the prey of a persecution mania that only increased with the years! It seemed to him that the whole world was leagued against him; and in his solitude and excitement, his imagination wove the absurd web of a universal conspiracy; in its centre he believed he saw an unknown power – a power he avoided naming – which was bent upon causing him to suffer the most frightful tortures.

He sought and found temporary refuge in the land of the king of Prussia, in the district of Neuchâtel – although he found it distasteful to be under obligation to Frederick II for whom he felt an aversion – in this differing greatly from the French philosophers who fawned upon him (it is remarkable that the solitary dreamer had in political matters a much surer judgment than Voltaire). He took up his domicile in Motiers, in the Val-Travers, on June 9, 1762, and remained there two and a half years under the protection of the Prussian king's intelligent governor, Lord Keith (Lord Marshal) – such great noblemen, independent of opinion and personally enlightened, were always Rousseau's best defenders. But he lost this support by the departure of Marshal Keith and, with extreme imprudence, at the very moment he should have contrived to be forgotten, he gaily re-entered the battle with his *Lettres écrites de la Montagne* (June to October 1764), in which he strongly attacked his enemies, the Church and State of Geneva, and in which in the name of true Christianity he made the case against the Pharisees of reformed Protestantism.

All the pastors rose up in arms. The temple of Motiers was closed to him, communion refused, he was denounced from the pulpit as the Antichrist, the people were aroused against him, in the fields stones were thrown at him, he was threatened with a gun. In September 1765, a nocturnal attack on his house forced him to leave precipitately, and after a month's stay on the Île de St. Pierre, in the lake of Bienne, where he would have liked to pass the rest of his days (he wrote an account of this too brief sojourn in one of the most beautiful of the *Rêveries du Promeneur Solitaire*), Berne ordered him to leave. Again he had to fly, to fly from Switzerland, his fatherland, which repudiated him and which he now called a "murderous land."

He crossed Paris where he did not have the right to remain, and accepting the invitation extended him by the English historian David Hume, crossed to England, to London (January 1766), then to Wootton in Derbyshire. But Hume and Rousseau were little able to understand one another ; and Hume, by his ironical coldness, his ambiguous attitude and his hidden dealings with the greatest English and French enemies of his guest, alarmed and then maddened the morbidly sensitive Rousseau. He imagined in Hume one of the agents in the conspiracy against him ; and Hume's culpable indiscretion in unhesitatingly handing over to the implacable animosity of the Encyclopedists and the malevolence of the entire world, the secret of the derangement and the confidences of Rousseau, justified the suspicions of the latter.

This last blow distracted the poor delirious brain. In a panic of terror, he fled from England (May

1767), across France from place to place, like a hunted man.* At the height of his madness he ended each of his letters with the cry: "*I am innocent!*" He was allowed to return to Paris where he took up lodging in a poor house on the rue Plâtrière, earning his living as a copyist of music.

He had written his *Confessions*; the last page is pure madness; and he had read it to several friends. But they, fearing to be denounced – and Madame d'Epinay first among them – caused his readings to be forbidden by the police; and the *cabinet noir* intercepted his letters. This was not the way to calm his frenzy! Alone – "*More alone in the midst of Paris than Robinson on his island*" – believing himself spied upon as the enemy of the entire world, Rousseau wrote his hallucinated *Dialogues de Rousseau avec Jean-Jacques*, the most piercing analysis he ever made of himself, but giving the wildest account of the conspiracy against him. Imagining no human being capable of hearing his despairing cry, he called out to God, and decided to deliver his manuscript directly to Him, by laying it on the high altar of Notre Dame in Paris. He found the grill to the choir closed! This was the supreme blow. It seemed to him that God Himself had turned against him. . .†

* He thought of fleeing to America, to the islands of the Archipelago, to Cyprus, or any other forgotten corner of Greece, under the protection of the Grand Turk, safe from the "cruelty of Christian charity." (Letter of Oct. 5, 1768.)

As a matter of fact he was still under the decree of arrest; and his friends, even the Prince de Conti, was worried. He had to change his name.

† He also caused to be printed a great many copies of an appeal: "To all Frenchmen who still love justice and truth"; and distributed them in the streets. In April 1776, he remitted

Then his deep piety convinced him that if God permitted him to be persecuted, that persecution must then have been written "*in the eternal decrees*," and there was nothing more for him to do but bow before them, sorrowfully but with confidence. . .

He was thus calmed, but his mental health was not restored. And the last work that occupied him, *Les Rêveries du Promeneur Solitaire* (begun in the autumn of 1776, and interrupted by his death in 1778), showed him no less mad than the *Dialogues*, but a tranquil madman, tender and sad, wandering in his mind. He was no longer irritated, it seemed to him he was living in a nightmare (and it was too true!), he awaited with resignation the hour when he would awaken. Now he knew, he believed, that he could look forward to no reparation on earth. . . "*Here I am alone on the earth, no brother, neighbor, friend, society, save myself. The most sociable and the most loving of human beings has been proscribed by unanimous accord.*" He was alone, eternally, "*calm at the bottom of the abyss, poor mortal, unfortunate, but impassive like God himself. . .*"

Nevertheless, his art had lost nothing; it was even purified. And these last *Rêveries* are like the beautiful song of an old and melancholy nightingale in the silence of the forest. He mulls over the few happy days of his life: they were above all those in which he was absorbed into nature, one with the Cosmos. More than any man of the West, he realized complete ecstasy in the Oriental sense, "*the feeling*

the manuscript of the *Dialogues* to a young English visitor, who seemed to him to have been sent from heaven; and this friend had the work printed in London in 1780. The original is in the British Museum.

of being stripped bare of any other affection," that concentration in the depths of Being, "*in which he was entwined with himself.*" The great relaxation of his last days was botany : what he most liked in this was not the satisfaction of scientific knowledge, but contact with the life of the earth and all the memories it evoked, "*the fields, the water, the woods, solitude, above all, peace and rest. . .*" He also beguiled himself with music, with the melodies he sang. They were later collected under the title : *Les Consolations des Misères de ma Vie.*

For the last month of his life, he was lucky enough to be taken away from his poor Paris lodging and transported to the most beautiful of country places, Ermenonville, nine leagues from the capital, by the generosity of a rich gentleman, M. de Girardin. He was installed here on May 20, 1778, and he fully enjoyed this little paradise regained. Even his health seemed improved. At the end of June, an English visitor, H. de Magellan, heard him accompany on the piano the *canzonetta* "Saul," in *Othello,* which was the last of his compositions. On Thursday morning, July 2, 1778, he was stricken. The doctors diagnosed a cerebral œdema – "*ictus apoplectique consécutif à grand urémie.*" *

The unfortunate man, who in dying thought himself "*alone on the earth*" and condemned to remain

* A study by Dr. S. Elosu, *La maladie de J. J. Rousseau* (1929, Fischbacher), gives the best account of all of Rousseau's illnesses in the course of his life. It is the most complete and reasonable résumé of all that has been written on the subject.

Rousseau's enemies spread a rumor of suicide. This rumor should absolutely be rejected. All the testimony of the autopsy is conclusive. Moreover, Rousseau was profoundly opposed to suicide.

so "*for eternity*," did not know that he had conquered the present and the future. During the last years of his life, from 1770 to 1778, six editions of his complete works had appeared, ten of *La Nouvelle Héloïse.* In 1782 were published the first part of his *Confessions* and the *Rêveries* which excited the imagination of readers already intrigued by the mystery of his sudden death in the romantic setting of Ermenonville. From 1780, half of France made pilgrimage to the Île des Peupliers where rested the ashes of the mad sage – even the Queen and all the Princes. Visitors abandoned themselves to transports of adoration and love. In vain was the hatred of the "philosophers" shown by venomous attacks and attempts to destroy a reputation detracting from their own. All opposition was broken. The rising revolutionary generation invoked the republican of Geneva, who – in contrast to the great lord of Ferney, Voltaire, who died a month before (May 31, 1778) – faithful to his principles, had led to the end the life of a man of the people, a little country bourgeois. The future leaders of the French Revolution, of every party, who were later to devour one another – Barnace, Danton, Carnot, Billaud, Varenne, Coujon, Manon Roland – were united in the cult rendered Rousseau. Brissot went to the Bastille for having developed the consequences of the *Discours sur l'inégalité.* Robespierre, who had seen Rousseau during the last days of his life, consecrated his life to him in a sort of *ex-voto*, on the eve of his entrance into political action. He stressed Rousseau's teaching in the tribune, and, arrived at the height of his power, he exalted him in his famous speech of the 18th Floréal (May 7, 1794). In this oration he avenged Rousseau for the hostility of the *Encyclopedists*, paying him the homage of "*this Revolution of which he was the precursor, and which carried him to the Pantheon.*" He bestowed upon him, with the crown of oak leaves, "*the ministry of preceptor of the human race.*" In the hall of the Constituent Assembly, the bust of Jean-Jacques faced those of Franklin and of Washington.

But the influence of Rousseau extended beyond politics. It permeated and fructified German philosophy. Kant was overcome by reading *Emile*; he vowed he could never reread it without being transported. "*There was a time,*" he said, "*when I proudly imagined that knowledge constituted the honor of humanity, and I looked down upon the ignorant people. It was Rousseau who unsealed my eyes. This illusory superiority vanished: I learned to honor man.*" The *Contrat social* had no less an effect upon him. In it he found his own moral illumination, his principle of "*that liberty which is man's characteristic.*" Later the founders of Marxism, who appropriated the dialectics of Hegel, showed its workings by examples taken from Rousseau.

All the German geniuses of the great *Sturm und Drang* movement, beginning with Lessing, its precursor, and with Herder, down to Goethe and Schiller who composed an *Ode to Rousseau*, were members of the Rousseauan cult.

It was not only his thought which was revolutionary. His very writing brought about a revolution in the manner of feeling and of expressing feeling; and it transformed the art of the future. Rousseau was several men in one, several different artists, and all of the first order. He was a powerful orator, with no equal in France save Bossuet; without seeking to do so, he revived the eloquence of the classic Forum; certain of his writings are overwhelming orations. He had the harmony, the pitch, the burning flow of a Demosthenes.

And at the same time he was the master of an intimate art, of the reverie which speaks half-aloud, of the confession which pierces to the bottom of the soul. His psycho-physiological peculiarities, which were at once the cause of his genius and of his ills, were essentially derived from his egotism. With no regard for the usages of society or of modish literature, he spoke only of himself. He had discovered the real "*I*." He had worked, as he said, in the "*dark chamber*," with no other art than "*to follow exactly the lines which he saw marked.*" He was never tired of observing himself. Up to his time, no one had yet done this to the same degree, with the exception of Montaigne: Rousseau even taxed him with having posed for the public.

Now in thus shamelessly expressing himself, he stripped bare and exposed what thousands of beings of his time were forced to repress. He freed the modern soul, he taught it to burst its fetters, to know and express itself.

We may add that, in order to express this new world, he had to create a new language, which was free and more supple.

"*I choose my own style as I choose other things. I do not try to make it uniform; I will always have that which comes to me, I will use it as I like, without scruple; I will say each thing that I feel, as I see it, without studied effect, without constraint, with-*

out worrying myself about the mixture. In throwing myself into the memory of the impression received and of the feeling that is present, I will give a double painting of the state of my soul; namely at the moment the event took place, and at the moment I describe it: my uneven and natural style, at times rapid and at others diffuse, sometimes wise and sometimes mad, sometimes grave and again gay, will itself form a part of my story. . ."

This richness of rhythm and emotion might easily have degenerated into confusion, if the born musician within him had not held the baton of orchestra chief. He wrote in 1760 to his printer Rey that he was above all a musician for whom "*harmony was of so great importance in style that he placed it immediately after clarity, and even before accuracy.*" If the need arose, he would have sacrificed to it the truthfulness of the story; he deliberately sacrificed grammar in order not to compromise harmony. With him, ideas came after rhythm. He first sang within himself his periods and his sentences, without giving them words. Without doubt he was a great prose poet and a precursor of French romanticism, no less by his meter and rhythm than by his sensitiveness and his ideas. Chateaubriand and Lamartine sprang from him. Michelet and George Sand were impregnated with Rousseau.

All modern pedagogic theory is inspired by his *Emile* and his knowledge of the child. The most celebrated institute of new education in Geneva bears his name. He, so weak toward himself, proved an admirable director of conscience, firm and lucid, without harshness. He had a generous instinct for true morality, sane and alive, not dogmatic nor abstract, nor subject to any principles or *Credo*, but adapted to just needs and weaknesses, profoundly humane.

A thing both singular and remarkable in a mind so classic, disposed toward absolute judgments, his rigor as a maker of rules was entirely imbued by a relativism that is modern and in accord with his passion for tolerance. In his *Lettre à D'Alembert* will be found clearly stated the principle of relative right, of the relativity of judgment and of historical relativism. He had an acute sense of movement, of πάντα ῥεῖ and by this dynamism, contrasting with the static rationalism of preceding times, he prepared the way for modern thought, for the "Die and become !" (*Stirb und Werde !*) of Goethe.

He opened into literature the riches of the subconscious, the secret movements of being, hitherto ignored and repressed, and their constant fermentations, the *libido*. He was one of the sources of Freudianism.

From him, Tolstoi received the thunderbolt in his youth. As a young man he wore about his neck a medal bearing Rousseau's portrait, like a holy image. His moral reform and his school of Iasnaia Poliana were based upon the teachings and example of Jean-Jacques. To his last days, he continued to invoke him. Their resemblance is no less striking in the field of art than that of religion. "*So much do the pages of Rousseau touch my heart*," said Tolstoi, "*I believe that I might have written them.*" In truth, he did re-write them. He was the Jean-Jacques of our day.

Rousseau has not ceased his influence upon modern thought. Young Japan, the new China, have harbored his teachings.

May I be permitted, in ending, to speak of my personal gratitude to the great musician-poet. I have often encountered his shade in my walks about the shore of beautiful Lake Leman "*around which*," he wrote, "*his heart has never ceased to roam*" – and from the window of the dwelling at Villeneuve where I write these lines, I see the bay and slopes of Clarens ; at its summit, between the trees, the rose-colored house of Julie stands dreaming.

Romain Rolland has selected and arranged the essence of Rousseau's work from

DISCOURSE ON THE ORIGIN OF INEQUALITIES
LETTER TO D'ALEMBERT
THE REVERIES OF A SOLITARY WALKER
THE SOCIAL CONTRACT
EMILE
JULIE
THE CONFESSIONS

THE WORKS OF

JEAN-JACQUES ROUSSEAU

(1712–1778)

Discourse on the Arts and Sciences (1749)
The Village Soothsayer (1753)
Discourse on the Origin of Inequality (1753)
Letter on French Music (1753)
Letter to D'Alembert on the Theatre (1758)
Discourse on Political Economy (1758)
Julie, or The New Héloïse (1761)
The Social Contract (1762)
Emile, or Education (1762)
The Confessions (1765–1770)
The Reveries of a Solitary Walker (1778)

ROUSSEAU'S DISCOURSES

Of the three Discourses of Jean-Jacques Rousseau — the first, upon the Arts and Sciences (1749) ; *the second, upon the Origin of Inequalities among Mankind* (1753) ; *the third (Letter to D'Alembert), upon the Theatre* (1758) : *the first, although it created the greatest excitement and founded the reputation of Jean-Jacques, is by far the most superficial. One feels that it was written in a few hours, literally to have flowed from the pen; and despite the author's state of exaltation while writing it, it gives the impression of being a paradoxical play of the mind, similar to the philosophical literature of the salons. Jean-Jacques does not yet appear to have entirely understood the seriousness of the question, nor above all to have taken his own powers fully into account. He only shows the distrust and dislike of a young provincial Genevese toward Parisian society, against the* "treacherous uniformity" *it imposed, and against* "the perfidious veil of politeness" *which surrounded it. He reproached science, letters and art with having allowed themselves to be dominated and tamed by power and of* "spreading garlands of flowers over the iron chains with which men are laden." *His criticisms of these things lacked weight. Although his Discourse appeared to be only an exercise in oratory for the diversion of men of letters, it also threatened to lead ill-adjusted minds to dangerous excesses: thus for example, the condemna-*

tion of the printing press and of the "frightful disorders" *it caused — which led to the logical conclusion that the libraries too must be burned. If Jean-Jacques later complained that his first Discourse was ill understood, and gave added explanations of his thesis, it can also be said that the Discourse of* 1749 *readily lent itself to misunderstanding.*

The first Discourse was, besides, too literary and not solid enough to cause anxiety. It could be attributed to a young and brilliant college "rhetorician" who set forth his prosopopoeia in the style of a Latin discourse. It is that success which, revealing to Jean-Jacques the power of his pen, inspired him with a just pride in his extraordinary personality ; and he finally dared "to appear as he really was." *Between the first and the second Discourse, he became another man who boldly threw down the gauntlet to the society of his day.*

The second Discourse upon a question proposed by the Academy of Dijon, "What is the origin of inequality among men, and is it authorized by natural law ?" *is dedicated to the Republic of Geneva ; and the dedication contains, together with a eulogy of the Republic, the ideal picture of the country and government under which Jean-Jacques would wish to live.*

A DISCOURSE

ON A SUBJECT PROPOSED BY THE ACADEMY OF DIJON:

WHAT IS THE ORIGIN OF INEQUALITY AMONG MEN, AND IS IT AUTHORISED BY NATURAL LAW?

I conceive that there are two kinds of inequality among the human species; one, which I call natural or physical, because it is established by nature, and consists in a difference of age, health, bodily strength, and the qualities of the mind or of the soul: and another, which may be called moral or political inequality, because it depends on a kind of convention, and is established, or at least authorised by the consent of men. This latter consists of the different privileges, which some men enjoy to the prejudice of others; such as that of being more rich, more honoured, more powerful or even in a position to exact obedience.

The subject of the present discourse, therefore, is more precisely this. To mark, in the progress of things, the moment at which right took the place of violence and nature became subject to law, and to explain by what sequence of miracles the strong came to submit to serve the weak, and the people to purchase imaginary repose at the expense of real felicity.

There is a very specific quality which distinguishes man from the brute and which will admit of no dispute. This is the faculty of self-improvement, which, by the help of circumstances, gradually develops all the rest of our faculties, and is inherent in the species as in the individual. In all the nations of the world, the progress of the understanding has been exactly proportionate to the wants which the peoples had received from nature, or been subjected to by circumstances, and in consequence to the passions that induced them to provide for those necessities.

The more we reflect on this subject, it is impossible indeed to conceive how a man, by his own powers alone, without the aid of communication and the spur of necessity, could have bridged so great a gap.

I think I need not fear contradiction in holding man to be possessed of the only natural virtue, which could not be denied him by the most violent detractor of human virtue. I am speaking of compassion, which is a disposition suitable to creatures so weak and subject to so many evils as we certainly are : by so much the more universal and useful to mankind, as it comes before any kind of reflection ; and at the same time so natural, that the very brutes themselves sometimes give evident proofs of it.

In spite of all their morality, men would have never been better than monsters, had not nature bestowed on them a sense of compassion, to aid their reason : but he did not see that from this quality alone flow all those social virtues, of which he denied man the possession. But what is generosity, clemency or humanity but compassion applied to the weak, to the guilty, or to mankind in general ? Even benevolence and friendship are, if we judge rightly, only the effects of compassion, constantly set upon a particular object : for how is it different to wish that another person may not suffer pain and uneasiness and to wish him happy? Compassion must, in fact, be the stronger, the more the animal beholding any kind of distress identifies himself with the animal that suffers. Now, it is plain that such identification must have been much more perfect in a state of nature than it is in a state of reason. It is reason that engenders self-respect, and reflection that confirms it: it is reason which turns man's mind back upon itself, and divides him from everything that could disturb or afflict him.

It is then certain that compassion is a natural feeling, which, by moderating the violence of love of self in each individual, contributes to the preservation of the whole species. It is this compassion that hurries us without reflection to the relief of those who are in distress: it is this which in a state of nature supplies the place of laws, morals and virtues, with the advantage that none are tempted to disobey its gentle voice.

The inequality of mankind is hardly felt in a state of nature.

The first man who, having enclosed a piece of ground, bethought himself of saying *This is mine*, and found people simple enough to believe him, was the real founder of civil society. From how many crimes, wars and murders, from how many horrors and misfortunes might not any one have saved mankind, by pulling up the stakes, or filling up the ditch, and crying to his fellows, "Beware of listening to this impostor; you are undone if you once forget that the fruits of the earth belong to us all, and the earth itself to nobody." But there is great probability that things had then already come to such a pitch, that they could no longer continue as they were ; for the idea of property depends on many prior ideas, which could only be acquired successively, and cannot have been formed all at once in the human mind. Mankind must have made very considerable progress, and acquired considerable knowledge and industry which they must also have transmitted and increased from age to age, before they arrived at this last point of the state of nature.

From the moment one man began to stand in need of the help of another ; from the moment it appeared advantageous to any one man to have enough provisions for two, equality disappeared, property was introduced, work became indispensable, and vast forests became smiling fields, which man had to water with the sweat of his brow, and where slavery and misery were soon seen to germinate and grow up with the crops.

Metallurgy and agriculture were the two arts which produced this great revolution. The poets tell us it was gold and silver, but, for the philosophers, it was iron and corn, which first civilised men, and ruined humanity.

The cultivation of the earth necessarily brought about its distribution ; and property, once recognised, gave rise to the first rules of justice.

In this state of affairs, equality might have been sustained, had the talents of individuals been equal, and had, for example, the use of iron and the consumption of commodities always exactly balanced each other ; but, as there was nothing to preserve this balance, it was soon disturbed ; the strongest did most work ; the most skilful turned his labour to best account ; the most ingenious devised methods of diminishing his labour : the husbandman wanted more iron, or the smith more corn, and, while both laboured equally, the one gained a great deal by his work, while the other could hardly support himself. Thus natural inequality unfolds itself insensibly with that of combination.

On the other hand, free and independent as men were before, they were now, in consequence of a multiplicity of new wants, brought into subjection, as it were, to all nature, and particularly to one another ; and each became in some degree a slave even in becoming the master of other men : if rich, they stood in need of the services of others ; if poor, of their assistance ; and even a middle condition did not enable them to do without one another. Man must now, therefore, have been perpetually employed in getting others to interest themselves in his lot, and in making them, apparently at least, if not really, find their advantage in promoting his own. Thus he must have been sly and artful in his behaviour to some, and imperious and cruel to others ; being under a kind of necessity to ill-use all the persons of whom he stood in need, when he could not frighten them into compliance, and did not judge it his interest to be useful to them. There arose rivalry and competition on the one hand, and conflicting interests on the other, together with a secret desire on both of profiting at the expense of others. All these evils were the first effects of property, and the inseparable attendants of growing inequality.

It is impossible that men should not at length have reflected on so wretched a situation, and on the calamities that overwhelmed them. The rich, in particular, must have felt how much they suffered by a constant state of war, of which they bore all the expense. Destitute of valid reasons to justify and sufficient strength to defend himself, able to crush individuals with ease, but easily crushed himself by a troop of bandits, one against all, and incapable, on account of mutual jealousy, of joining with his equals against numerous enemies united by the common hope of plunder, the rich man, thus urged by necessity, conceived at length the profoundest plan that ever entered the mind of man : this was to employ in his favour the forces of those who attacked him, to make allies of his adversaries, to inspire them with different maxims, and to give them other institutions as favourable to himself as the law of nature was unfavourable.

With this view, after having represented to his neighbours the horror of a situation which armed every man against the rest, and made their possessions as burdensome to them as their wants, and in which no safety could be expected either in riches or in poverty, he readily devised plausible arguments to make them close with his design. "Let us join," said he, "to guard the weak from oppression, to restrain the ambitious, and secure to every man the possession of what belongs to him : let us institute rules of justice and peace, to which all without exception may be obliged to conform ; rules that may in some measure make amends for the caprices of fortune, by subjecting equally the powerful and the weak to the observance of reciprocal obligations. Let us, in a word, instead of turning our forces against ourselves, collect them in a supreme power which may govern us by wise laws.

All ran headlong to their chains, in hopes of securing their liberty ; for they had just wit enough to perceive the advantages of political institutions, without experience enough to enable them to foresee the dangers. The most capable of foreseeing the dangers were the very persons who expected to benefit by them.

Such was, or may well have been, the origin of society and law, which bound new fetters on the poor, and gave new powers to the rich ; which irretrievably destroyed natural liberty, eternally fixed the law of property and inequality, converted clever usurpation into unalterable right, and, for the advantage of a few ambitious individuals, subjected all mankind to perpetual labour, slavery and wretchedness. It is easy to see how the establishment of one community made that of all the rest necessary, and how, in order to make head against united forces, the rest of mankind had to unite in turn. Societies soon multiplied and spread over the face of the earth, till hardly a corner of the world was left in which a man could escape the yoke, and withdraw his head from beneath the sword which he saw perpetually hanging over him by a thread. Civil right having thus become the common rule among the members of each community, the law of nature maintained its place only between different communities, where, under the name of the right of nations, it was qualified by certain tacit conventions, in order to make commerce practicable, and serve as a substitute for natural compassion, which lost, when applied to societies, almost all the influence it had over individuals, and survived no longer except in some great cosmopolitan spirits, who, breaking down the imaginary barriers that separate different peoples, follow the example of our Sovereign Creator, and include the whole human race in their benevolence.

Hence arose national wars, battles, murders, and reprisals, which shock nature and outrage reason ; together with all those horrible prejudices which class among the virtues the honour of shedding human blood. The most distinguished men hence learned to consider cutting each other's throats a duty ; at length men massacred their fellow-creatures by thousands without so much as knowing why. Such were the first effects which we can see to have followed the division of mankind into different communities.

It is beyond dispute, and indeed the fundamental maxim of all political right, that people have set up chiefs to protect their liberty, and not to enslave them. *If we have a prince*, said Pliny to Trajan, *it is to save ourselves from having a master.*

I consider the establishment of the political body as a real contract between the people and the chiefs chosen by them : a contract by which both parties bind themselves to observe the laws therein expressed, which form the ties of their union. The people having in respect of their social relations concentrated all their wills in one, the several articles, concerning which this will is explained, become so many fundamental laws, obligatory on all the members of the State without exception, and one of these articles regulates the choice and power of the magistrates appointed to watch over the execution of the rest. This power extends to everything which may maintain the constitution, without going so far as to alter it.

If we follow the progress of inequality in these various revolutions, we shall find that the establishment of laws and of the right of property was its first term, the institution of magistracy the second, and the conversion of legitimate into arbitrary power the third and last ; so that the condition of rich and poor was authorised by the first period ; that of powerful and weak by the second ; and only by the third that of master and slave, which is the last degree of inequality, and the term at which all the rest remain, when they have got so far.

Political distinctions necessarily produce civil distinctions. These differences are of several kinds ; but riches, nobility or rank, power and personal merit being the principal distinctions by which men form an estimate of each other in society, I could prove that the harmony or conflict of these different forces is the surest indication of the good or bad constitution of a State. I could show that among these four kinds of inequality, personal qualities being the origin of all the others, wealth is the one to which they are all reduced in the end ; for, as riches tend most immediately to the prosperity of individuals, and are easiest to communicate, they are used to purchase every other distinction. By this observation we are enabled to judge pretty exactly how far a people has departed from its primitive constitution, and of its progress towards the extreme term of corruption.

If we exposed all the different aspects, under

which inequality has up to the present appeared, we should see oppression continually gain ground without it being possible for the oppressed to know where it would stop, or what legitimate means was left them of checking its progress. We should see the rights of citizens, and the freedom of nations slowly extinguished, and the complaints, protests and appeals of the weak treated as seditious murmurings. We should see the honour of defending the common cause confined by statecraft to a mercenary part of the people. We should see taxes made necessary by such means, and the disheartened husbandman deserting his fields even in the midst of peace, and leaving the plough to gird on the sword. We should see the champions of their country sooner or later becoming its enemies, and for ever holding their daggers to the breasts of their fellow-citizens.

It is from the midst of this disorder and these revolutions, that despotism, gradually raising up its hideous head and devouring everything that remained sound and untainted in any part of the State, would at length trample on both the laws and the people, and establish itself on the ruins of the republic. The times which immediately preceded this last change would be times of trouble and calamity ; but at length the monster would swallow up everything, and the people would no longer have either chiefs or laws, but only tyrants.

This is the last term of inequality, the extreme point that closes the circle, and meets that from which we set out. Here all private persons return to their first equality, because they are nothing ; and, subjects having no law but the will of their master, and their master no restraint but his passions, all notions of good and all principles of equity again vanish. There is here a complete return to the law of the strongest, and so to a new state of nature. The contract of government is so completely dissolved by despotism, that the despot is master only so long as he remains the strongest; as soon as he can be expelled, he has no right to complain of violence. The popular insurrection that ends in the death or deposition of a Sultan is as lawful an act as those by which he disposed, the day before, of the lives and fortunes of his subjects. As he was maintained by force alone, it is force alone that overthrows him. Thus everything takes place according to the natural order.

It follows from this survey that, as there is hardly any inequality in the state of nature, all the inequality which now prevails owes its strength and growth to the development of our faculties and the advance of the human mind, and becomes at last permanent and legitimate by the establishment of property and laws. Secondly, it follows that moral inequality, authorised by positive right alone, clashes with natural right, whenever it is not proportionate to physical inequality; a distinction which sufficiently determines what we ought to think of that species of inequality which prevails in all civilised countries; since it is plainly contrary to the law of nature, however defined, that children should command old men, fools wise men, and that the privileged few should gorge themselves with superfluities, while the starving multitude are in want of the bare necessities of life.

J.-J. ROUSSEAU

CITIZEN OF GENEVA

to M. D'ALEMBERT

OF THE FRENCH ACADEMY, OF THE ROYAL ACADEMY OF SCIENCE OF PARIS, OF THAT OF PRUSSIA, OF THE ROYAL SOCIETY OF LONDON, OF THE ROYAL ACADEMY OF BELLES-LETTRES OF SWEDEN, AND OF THE INSTITUTE OF BOLOGNA

ON HIS ARTICLE

GENEVA

IN THE VII VOLUME OF THE ENCYCLOPEDIA
AND ESPECIALLY

ON THE PLAN TO ESTABLISH A THEATRE OF COMEDY
IN THIS CITY

PREFACE

Justice and truth are the first obligations of man: humanity, his country, are his first affections! When private considerations make him invert this order, he commits a crime.

Solitude calms the soul, and assuages those passions, which arise from the hurry and tumult of the world. Remote from the provocation of vice, we speak of it with less indignation: remote from the evils that affect us, we have less sensibility of heart. Since I no longer converse with mankind, I have almost ceased to detest the wicked. Besides, the ill they have done me deprives me of all right to say any harm of them: henceforward must I forgive them, that there may be no resemblance between us.

I should substitute, without further thought, the love of reverence to that of justice : but it is much better to forget everything.

I think I have found a principle, which if fully demonstrated as it may be, would instantly disarm persecution and superstition, and assuage that fury for making proselytes, which seems to animate the ignorant. It is that human reason hath no common determinate measure, and that it is very wrong for any man to lay down his own sense of things as a rule for others.

Let us suppose the disputants to be sincere ; otherwise all they say is idle prate. So far as a certain point there are common principles, and common evidence ; and besides, each man has his own reason to determine him ; therefore his opinion does not lead to scepticism ; but, on the other hand, as the general limits of reason are not fixed, and no man has a power or control over the understanding of another person, the proud dogmatism must be stopped short. If ever peace could be established, where interest, pride, and ambition reign at present, the quarrels of priests and philosophers would have an end.

But what method would you point out for keeping men within bounds ? Severe laws, well executed. Severe laws, you say ! The first is to suffer no such : if we violate this, what will become of the severity of the rest ? Laws well executed ? The question is whether that can be done : for the force of laws has its measure, and so has that of vice. We cannot be sure of executing the laws, till we have compared these two quantities, and find that the former surpasseth the latter. The knowledge of these two relations constitutes the proper science of a legislator: for if his business was no more than to publish edicts and regulations, with a view of redressing abuses as fast as they rise, no doubt but he would say very fine things; yet for the most part they would be ineffectual, and serve rather as hints towards excellent laws, than as a means to execute them. Upon the whole, the framing of laws is not such a great matter, but every sensible honest man may very well hit upon such institutions, as, when properly observed, shall be of great use to society. Where is the least student of the law, that is not capable to draw up a moral code as pure as that of Plato's republic? But that is not the only point in debate. The business is to suit this code in such a manner to the people for whom it is framed, and to the matters ordained therein, that the execution thereof shall follow naturally from the sole concurrence of these relations; which is, following Solon's example, in compiling such laws, as are not indeed the best in themselves but the best the people can bear and in such and such circumstances: otherwise it is much better that disorders should continue, than be prevented or provided against by laws, which are not to be observed; for besides not redressing the evil, it is exposing the law to contempt.

Another, and not less important, observation is that matters of morality and universal justice, are not regulated like those of particular justice and strict right, by laws and edicts: or if the laws have sometimes an influence on manners, it is when they derive their whole force from that spring. In such a case they return that very force, by a kind of reaction well known to true politicians.

How then can government have an influence on manners? My answer is, by the public opinion. As our habits arise from our opinions in retirement, in society they are owing to those of others. When we live in society, it is the judgment of our fellow-members that determines our actions: nothing appears good or desirable to private people, but what the public has judged such; and the only happiness most men know, is to be esteemed happy.

With regard to the choice of proper means for directing the public opinion, this is another question – and this is not the proper place to resolve it. These means are neither laws nor punishments, nor any sort of coercive methods.

Therefore it is all in vain; neither reason, nor virtue, nor laws will prevail over the public opinion, so long as there is no contrivance to change it. Once more I say it, force will not do.

Opinion, queen of the world, is in no wise subject to the power of kings; they themselves are her first slaves.

If a government can greatly influence the manners of the people, it is only by its primitive institution: when once it has determined those manners, not only it has no longer the power to alter them, unless it undergoes a revolution itself; but it will find a very great difficulty in preserving them against the unavoidable accidents by which they are continually attacked, and their natural bias to change. Public opinions, though so difficult to govern, are in themselves of a very mutable nature. Chance, a thousand fortuitous causes, and unforeseen circumstances, will bring about what force and reason cannot; or rather, it is because chance directs them that force is ineffectual: just as in a throw of dice, let the impulse of the hand be never so strong, it will not be in the least the more effectual towards hitting the lucky point.

The most that human wisdom can do, is to prevent changes, and carefully to guard against everything that is likely to produce them; but as soon as they are suffered or authorised, it is very seldom that the magistrates can control and indeed they are never sure of controlling their effects.

In monarchies, never can private wealth raise a man above the prince; but in a republic it may easily set him above the laws. Then the government has no longer any weight, and the rich man is the real sovereign.

Must there be then, say you, no shows nor sports in a republic? Yes, there must and a great many. It is republics that first instituted them, and it is in republics that they are exhibited with a genuine air of festivity. Who are the people, whom it most becomes to have frequent meetings, and to enter into agreeable parties of pleasure and mirth, but they who have so many reasons to love each other, and to continue for ever united? We have many of these public festivals already; and were we to have more, I should still be pleased. But let us not adopt those exclusive entertainments which hold only a small number of people, locked up, as it were, in a gloomy cavern, where they sit timid and motionless in pensive silence; where the eye is offended with such disagreeable objects, as partition walls, iron spikes, soldiers, and striking images of servitude and inequality. No, happy people, these are not your festivals! You are to assemble in the open air, under the canopy of heaven, and there you are to feast on the contemplation of your happiness. Let your pleasures be neither mercenary nor effeminate; let no constraint nor interest adulterate them; let them be free and generous like yourselves; let the sun dart its rays on your innocent spectacles, and then you will form one yourselves, the finest that eyes can behold.

But you want to know the nature of these festivals, and what is to be shown there: nothing, if you will. Wherever liberty and affluence reign, there is the seat of true happiness. You may plant a maypole in the middle of a square and crown it with flowers; let the people then be assembled round, and this shall be called a festival. You may do better still: let the spectators be exhibited as a show; let them be actors themselves; let each man see and love himself in others, to the end that they may be all the more intimately united. I have no occasion to refer to the games of the ancient Greeks; there are others of modern date, which still exist, and are in use with us. Every year we have reviews, and public prizes, such as the crowning of those who are excellent in shooting at a mark, or in artillery and navigation. Institutions so useful,* and so agreable, cannot be

* It is not enough that the people have bread, and live according to their station; they must also live agreably; to the end that they may be more able to discharge their respective duties, and less eager to alter their condition; as also that the public order may be the better established. Good morals depend more than we imagine, on every man's being pleased with his condition of life. Briguing and intrigues are owing to restlessness and discontent: everything goes amiss, when one person covets another's employment. To do well in life, a man

too numerous ; there cannot be too many coronations of this sort. Why should not we do as much to render ourselves hearty and robust, as to learn the military exercise ? Hath the republic less need of artists than soldiers ? Why should not we, on the plan of the military rewards, found other gymnastic prizes, for wrestling, for races, for the disc, and for various bodily exercise ? Why should not we excite our watermen by rowing for wagers on the lake ? Can there be in the universe a more splendid sight than to behold a hundred boats, elegantly rigged, on that spacious magnificent basin, putting off at a signal given, in order to seize a flag hoisted at a mark, and attending on the victor to receive the merited prize ?

I gave the feasts of the Lacedemonians as a model of those, which I should be glad to see established

---

must love his profession. The state is never rightly fixed, till each individual being seated in his place, their whole force is united, and concurs to the general good, instead of being employed to their mutual prejudice, as it must happen in every ill constituted government. This being premissed, what are we to think of those who would deprive the people of festivals, pleasures, and every kind of amusement, as tending to divert them from their work ? This maxim is barbarous, is false. So much the worse, if the people have no time left but to earn their bread : they must be allowed some to eat it in comfort ; otherwise they will not earn it long. That just and beneficent Deity, who is willing they should work, is willing also they should divert themselves : nature equally subjects them to exercise and repose, to pleasure and pain. The dislike to work hurts the poor wretches more than work itself. Therefore if you would have people active and industrious, give them festivals, give them amusements, which shall render them fond of their condition of life, and hinder their envying those of an easier situation. A few days lost in this manner, will enhance the value of the rest. Preside over their pleasures, in order to render them decent ; this is the right method to encourage them to work.

among fellow-citizens. It was not only their object, but likewise their simplicity that recommended them : there was no pomp, no luxury, or parade ; a secret charm of patriotism rendered them engaging, and they breathed a kind of military spirit becoming free men : * engaged neither in business, nor pleasures, or at least what are so called with us, they

* I remember when I was a boy, to have been struck with a very simple sight, which has been imprinted ever since in my memory, notwithstanding the length of time, and the multiplicity of other objects. The regiment of St. Gervais had performed their exercise, and according to custom they sat down to supper in companies ; most of the regiment met after supper in the Square of St. Gervais, and all went dancing, officers and soldiers together, round the fountain, on the basin of which there were drums, fifes, and men with flambeaus in their hands. When people have been exhilarated with feasting, their dancing does not seem to offer anything very enjoying to the eye ; and yet the concerted motion of five or six hundred men in uniform holding one another by the hand, and forming a long band, which winded in cadence, and without the least confusion, with a thousand turns and returns, a thousand sorts of figured evolutions, the choice songs that spirited them, the noise of drums, the light of flambeaus, and a certain military pomp amidst a scene of pleasure, all this together formed a very agreable spectacle, which it was impossible not to be affected with. It was late, the women were gone to bed ; they all got up. The windows were soon full of female gapers, who inspired the actors with fresh ardour ; but they could not confine themselves long to their windows, they came down ; the wives flocked about their husbands ; the servants brought wine, and the children, awakened by the noise ran half naked to their fathers and mothers. The dance was suspended ; nothing now passed but embracing, laughing, healths, caresses. From all this there resulted a general rapture, which I cannot describe, and which, in times of universal joy, we naturally feel, when surrounded by everything dear to us. My father embracing me, was seized with a palpitation which I think I feel and share with him still. "John," said he to me, "love thy country. See here thy honest countrymen ; they are all friends, all brothers ; joy and concord are in their hearts. Thou art a Genevois ; some time or other thou wilt see other people ; but

passed, in that delightful uniformity, the whole day without finding it too long, and their whole life without finding it too short. Each evening they came home, gay and good humoured, to take their frugal repast, content with their country, with their fellow-citizens, and with themselves. If you desire an example of these public diversions, I will give you one mentioned by Plutarch. There were, he says, three companies of dancers, according to the three several ages of nature, and each company made a chorus to the dance. That of the old men began the first, singing the following couplet:

> That active courage youthful blood contains
> Did once with equal vigour warm our veins.

Next came that of the young men, who sang in their turn, beating their arms in cadence:

> Valiant and bold we are, let who will try:
> Who dare accept our challenge, soon shall die.

---

when thou hast travelled as far as thy father, thou wilt say thou never didst see their fellows."

They wanted to recommence the dance, but it was no longer possible: they did not so much as know what they were doing; their heads were all turned with an inebriation sweeter far than that of wine. After staying some time on the square to laugh and chat, they were obliged to separate: each retired quietly with his family; and thus it was that those amiable prudent women brought back their husbands, not by disturbing, but going to share their pleasures. I am very sensible that this sight, which so greatly affected me, would have had no charm to a thousand others: one must have eyes made on purpose to see it, and a heart to feel it. No, there is no pure joy, but that of a community; and the genuine sentiments of nature are felt only by the people. O dignity, daughter of pride, and parent of corroding care, did ever thy gloomy slaves taste such a moment as this in all their lives?

Afterwards came the children, who answered them, singing with a loud voice :

> Those seeds which nature in our breast did sow,
> Shall soon to generous fruits of virtue grow :
> Then all those valiant deeds, which you relate,
> We will excel, and scorn to imitate.

These, Sir, are the entertainments proper for republics.

THE REVERIES OF A SOLITARY WALKER

Everything on earth is in a continual ebb. Nothing can keep a fixed and constant form ; and our affections, attached to external things, necessarily change with them. Always before or behind us, they recall the past, which is no more, or anticipate the future, which perhaps will never be : in all there is nothing solid to which the heart can cleave. Neither have we here below scarcely any other than passing pleasure ; as to continual happiness, I doubt if it is known. There is hardly a single instant of our liveliest enjoyments of which the heart can truly say, *I wish this instant would last for ever*. And how then can we call a fugitive state happy, which leaves uneasiness and void in the heart, which leaves regret for something preceding, and hope for something after it ?

But if there is a state in which the soul finds a seat solid enough entirely to repose and collect there its whole being, without being obliged to have recourse to the past, or stretch towards the future ; where time is to her a void ; where the present continually lasts, without, however, denoting its duration, and without the least sign of succession, without any other sense of privation or enjoyment, of pleasure or pain, hope or fear, than solely that of our existence, and that that sentiment alone is able wholly to occupy it ; as long as that state lasts, he who finds himself in it may call himself happy, not from a poor, imperfect, relative happiness, like that we feel in the pleasures of life, but from a full, perfect, and sufficient happiness, which does not leave the least void in the soul it would be glad to fill. This is the state in which I often found myself on St. Peter's island, during my solitary reveries, whether stretched in my boat, seated on the shores of the agitated lake, or else on the banks of a beautiful river, or a brook murmuring through the gravel.

In what consists the enjoyment of a like situation? In nothing external, nothing but one's self, and our own existence; as long as this state lasts, we are sufficient to ourselves, like God. The sense of existence, stripped of every other affection, is of itself a precious sense of contentment and peace, which alone would suffice to render this existence lovely and sweet, to him who knows to remove from his mind all those terrestrial and sensual impressions which incessantly arise to distract and to trouble our comfort here below. But the greatest part of mankind, agitated by continual passions, are little acquainted with this state, and, having imperfectly tasted it a few moments, preserve an obscure and confused idea of it only, which does not enable them to feel its charms.

It is necessary the heart should be at peace, and that no passion arises to trouble the calm. It is necessary he who feels it should have dispositions adapted to it; they are likewise necessary in the concourse of surrounding objects. It does not demand an absolute repose, or too great an agitation, but an uniform and moderate movement, without fits or intervals. Without motion, life is a lethargy. If the movement is unequal or too violent, it awakens; in shewing us surrounding objects, it destroys the charms of thought and tears us from ourselves, instantly to restore us to the bonds of fortune and man, and brings us back to a sense of our misfortunes. An absolute silence leads to sadness : it represents the image of death. Then the succour of a happy imagination is necessary, and offers itself naturally enough to those who have received that blessing from Heaven. The movements, which do not externally arise, are then felt within us.

On awakening from any long and peaceful reverie, perceiving myself surrounded by flowers, birds, and verdure, permitting my wandering sight to rove remote over romantic shores, by which a vast extent of waters clear and crystalline was shut in, I assimilated every lovely object to my fictions, and, having at last a knowledge of myself, and that which surrounded me, I was unable to guess the point which separated fiction from reality ; so much did all combine to render dear the retired and solitary life I led in my beloved abode.

THE SOCIAL CONTRACT

In his Discourse on the Origin of Inequalities among Mankind (1753), *Rousseau put down as demonstrated the establishment* "of a true contract between the people and the leaders chosen by them," *but he added that he would postpone until later* "investigations still to be made upon the nature of the fundamental pact of all government."

Hardly was he installed in his Hermitage at Montmorency, in April 1756, *when he resumed these investigations. They seemed to him the most important of the tasks assigned to him. He said this in his* Confessions, *Book IX.* "*Of the various works which I had planned, the one I had considered the longest, which appealed most strongly to my taste, on which I wanted to work all my life, and which in my opinion should have placed the seal upon my reputation, was my* Political Institutions. . . *I conceived the first idea of the book thirteen or fourteen years ago when I was at Venice. . . Since that time my views had been greatly enlarged by the historical study of morals* [i. e. mainly by his *Discourse on the Origin of Inequalities*]. *I had come to see that in the last resort everything depends upon Politics; and that, whatever men may do, no nation will ever be anything but what the nature of its government may make it; thus the great question of the best possible government appears to me to be reduced to this: what is the nature of the government best adapted to train a nation to become the most virtu-*

ous, the most enlightened, the wisest, the best? . . . I thought I saw that this question was most closely united to this other question: what is the government which by its nature holds itself nearest to the law; from this question, what is the law? and a whole chain of questions of the same importance. I saw that all this led to great truths, useful for the happiness of humankind, but above all to that of my fatherland, where I had not found in the journey I had just made (1754) *notions of law and liberty that seemed to me sufficiently exact and clear. . .*"

He worked on this slowly, for several years, avoiding any mention of the work to anyone, even his then closest adviser — Diderot. He feared to introduce any spirit of satire into a work in which he intended "to put only the whole force of reason, without any trace of ill-humour or partiality." *After his* Letter to D'Alembert (1758), *he went back to his* Political Institutions, *but saw that it would take years to finish; he abandoned the project, extracting only* The Social Contract, *which he wrote at the same time he was engaged upon* Emile. The Social Contract *appeared in Amsterdam, one or two months before* Emile, *therefore in the spring of* 1762, *shortly before Rousseau's flight into Switzerland, where the works were burned at Geneva almost immediately after their appearance, on June* 18, 1762.

THE SOCIAL CONTRACT
OR
PRINCIPLES OF POLITICAL RIGHT

BOOK I

Man is born free ; and everywhere he is in chains.

Since no man has a natural authority over his fellow, and force creates no right, we must conclude that conventions form the basis of all legitimate authority among men.

We cannot invoke any voluntary alienation of liberty, as Grotius claims.

To renounce liberty is to renounce being a man, to surrender the rights of humanity and even its duties. Such a renunciation is incompatible with man's nature. The words *slave* and *right* contradict each other, and are mutually exclusive.

We must always go back to a first convention.

"The Social Compact" arises from the necessity of co-operation among men against natural forces.

"The problem is to find a form of association which will defend and protect with the whole common force the person and goods of each associate, and in which each, while uniting himself with all, may still obey himself alone, and remain as free as before." This is the fundamental problem of which the *Social Contract* provides the solution.

If we discard from the social compact what is

not of its essence, we shall find that it reduces itself to the following terms –

"Each of us puts his person and all his power in common under the supreme direction of the general will, and, in our corporate capacity, we receive each member as an indivisible part of the whole."

At once, in place of the individual personality of each contracting party, this act of association creates a moral and collective body, composed of as many members as the assembly contains votes, and receiving from this act its unity, its common identity, its life and its will. This public person, so formed by the union of all other persons, takes the name of sovereign.

As soon as this multitude is so united in one body, it is impossible to offend against one of the members without attacking the body, and still more to offend against the body without the members resenting it.

In order that the social compact may not be an empty formula, it tacitly includes the undertaking, which alone can give force to the rest, that whoever refuses to obey the general will shall be compelled to do so by the whole body. This means nothing less than that he will be forced to be free ; for this is the condition which, by giving each citizen to his country, secures him against all personal dependence.

What man loses by the social contract is his natural liberty and an unlimited right to everything he tries to get and succeeds in getting ; what he gains is civil liberty and the proprietorship of all he possesses.

We might add, to what man acquires in the civil state, moral liberty, which alone makes him truly master of himself ; for the mere impulse of appetite is slavery, while obedience to a law which we prescribe to ourselves is liberty.

I shall end this book by remarking on a fact on which the whole social system should rest : *i. e.* that, instead of destroying natural inequality, the fundamental compact substitutes, for such physical inequality as nature may have set up between men, an equality that is moral and legitimate, and that men, who may be unequal in strength or intelligence, become every one equal by convention and legal right.*

BOOK II

The first and most important deduction from the principles we have so far laid down is that the general will alone can direct the State according to the object for which it was instituted, *i. e.* the common good.

Sovereignty, being nothing less than the exercise of the general will, can never be alienated, and the Sovereign, who is no less than a collective being, cannot be represented except by himself.

The moment a master exists, there is no longer a Sovereign, and from that moment the body politic has ceased to exist.

Sovereignty, for the same reason as makes it inalienable, is indivisible ; for will either is, or is not,

* Under bad governments, this equality is only apparent and illusory : it serves only to keep the pauper in his poverty and the rich man in the position he has usurped. In fact, laws are always of use to those who possess and harmful to those who have nothing : from which it follows that the social state is advantageous to men only when all have something and none too much.

general; * it is the will either of the body of the people, or only of a part of it. In the first case, the will, when declared, is an act of Sovereignty and constitutes law: in the second, it is merely a particular will, or act of magistracy – at the most a decree.

It follows that the general will is always right and tends to the public advantage; but it does not follow that the deliberations of the people are always equally correct. Our will is always for our own good, but we do not always see what that is; the people is never corrupted, but it is often deceived, and on such occasions only does it seem to will what is bad.

There is often a great deal of difference between the will of all and the general will; the latter considers only the common interest, while the former takes private interest into account, and is no more than a sum of particular wills.

As nature gives each man absolute power over all his members, the social compact gives the body politic absolute power over all its members also; and it is this power which, under the direction of the general will, bears, as I have said, the name of Sovereignty.

Each man alienates, I admit, by the social compact, only such part of his powers, goods and liberty as it is important for the community to control; but it must also be granted that the Sovereign is sole judge of what is important.

Every service a citizen can render the State he ought to render as soon as the Sovereign demands it;

* To be general, a will need not always be unanimous; but every vote must be counted: any exclusion is a breach of generality.

but the Sovereign, for its part, cannot impose upon its subjects any fetters that are useless to the community, nor can it even wish to do so ; for no more by the law of reason than by the law of nature can anything occur without a cause.

We can see from this that the sovereign power, absolute, sacred and inviolable as it is, does not and cannot exceed the limits of general conventions, and that every man may dispose at will of such goods and liberty as these conventions leave him ; so that the Sovereign never has a right to lay more charges on one subject than on another, because, in that case, the question becomes particular, and ceases to be within its competency.

The social treaty has for its end the preservation of the contracting parties. He who wills the end wills the means also, and the means must involve some risks, and even some losses. He who wishes to preserve his life at others' expense should also, when it is necessary, be ready to give it up for their sake. Furthermore, the citizen is no longer the judge of the dangers to which the law desires him to expose himself ; and when the prince says to him : "It is expedient for the State that you should die," he ought to die, because it is only on that condition that he has been living in security up to the present, and because his life is no longer a mere bounty of nature, but a gift made conditionally by the State.

The death-penalty inflicted upon criminals may be looked on in much the same light : it is in order that we may not fall victims to an assassin that we consent to die if we ourselves turn assassins.

Again, every malefactor, by attacking social rights, becomes on forfeit a rebel and a traitor to his country ; by violating its laws he ceases to be a member of it ; he even makes war upon it. In such a case the preservation of the State is inconsistent with his own, and one or the other must perish ; in putting the guilty to death, we slay not so much the citizen as an enemy.

We may add that frequent punishments are always a sign of weakness or remissness on the part of the government. There is not a single ill-doer who could not be turned to some good. The State has no right to put to death, even for the sake of making an example, anyone whom it can leave alive without danger.

[*Rousseau then examines the "laws which are, properly speaking, only the conditions of civil association" and of which the people ought to be the author.*]

Good laws are not those which are good in themselves, but those which are well made for that particular people.

A thousand nations have achieved earthly greatness, that could never have endured good laws ; even such as could have endured them could have done so only for a very brief period of their long history. Most peoples, like most men, are docile only in youth ; as they grow old they become incorrigible. When once customs have become established and prejudices inveterate, it is dangerous and useless to attempt their reformation ; the people, like the foolish and cowardly patients who rave at sight of the doctor, can no longer bear that anyone should lay hands on its faults to remedy them.

Useful revolutions are rare ; they are exceptions, the cause of which is always to be found in the particular constitution of the State concerned. They cannot even happen twice to the same people, for it can make itself free as long as it remains barbarous, but not when the civic impulse has lost its vigour. Then disturbances may destroy it, but revolutions cannot mend it : it needs a master, and not a liberator. Free peoples, be mindful of this maxim : "Liberty may be gained, but can never be recovered."

As nature has set bounds to the stature of a well-made man, and, outside those limits, makes nothing but giants or dwarfs, similarly, for the constitution of a State to be at its best, it is possible to fix limits that will make it neither too large for good government, nor too small for self-maintenance. In every body politic there is a *maximum* strength which it cannot exceed and which it only loses by increasing in size. Every extension of the social tie means its relaxation ; and, generally speaking, a small State is stronger in proportion than a great one.

If we ask in what precisely consists the greatest good of all, which should be the end of every system of legislation, we shall find it reduce itself to two main objects, liberty and equality – liberty, because all particular dependence means so much force taken from the body of the State, and equality, because liberty cannot exist without it.

I have already defined civil liberty ; by equality, we should understand, not that the degrees of power and riches are to be absolutely identical for everybody; but that power shall never be great enough for violence, and shall always be exercised by virtue of rank and law; and that, in respect of riches, no citizen shall ever be wealthy enough to buy another, and none poor enough to be forced to sell himself.*

BOOK III

The public force needs an agent of its own to bind it together and set it to work under the direction of the general will, to serve as a means of communication between the State and the Sovereign. Here we have what is, in the State, the basis of government, often wrongly confused with the Sovereign, whose minister it is.

What then is government? An intermediate body set up between the subjects and the Sovereign, to secure their mutual correspondence, charged with the execution of the laws and the maintenance of liberty, both civil and political.

Those who hold that the act, by which a people puts itself under a prince, is not a contract, are certainly right. It is simply and solely a commission, an employment, in which the rulers, mere officials of the Sovereign, exercise in their own name the power of which it makes them depositaries. This power it can limit, modify or recover at pleasure.

In the first place, the Sovereign may commit the

* If the object is to give the State consistency, bring the two extremes as near to each other as possible; allow neither rich men nor beggars. These two estates, which are naturally inseparable, are equally fatal to the common good; from the one come the friends of tyranny, and from the other tyrants. It is always between them that public liberty is put up to auction; the one buys, and the other sells.

charge of the government to the whole people or to the majority of the people, so that more citizens are magistrates than are mere private individuals. This form of government is called *democracy*.

Or it may restrict the government to a small number, so that there are more private citizens than magistrates ; and this is named *aristocracy*.

Lastly, it may concentrate the whole government in the hands of a single magistrate from whom all others hold their power. This third form is the most usual, and is called *monarchy*, or royal government.

If we take the term in the strict sense, there never has been a real democracy, and there never will be. It is against the natural order for the many to govern and the few to be governed. It is unimaginable that the people should remain continually assembled to devote their time to public affairs, and it is clear that they cannot set up commissions for that purpose without the form of administration being changed.

Besides, how many conditions that are difficult to unite does such a government presuppose ! First, a very small State, where the people can readily be got together and where each citizen can with ease know all the rest ; secondly, great simplicity of manners, to prevent business from multiplying and raising thorny problems ; next, a large measure of equality in rank and fortune, without which equality of rights and authority cannot long subsist ; lastly, little or no luxury – for luxury either comes of riches or makes them necessary ; it corrupts at once rich and poor, the rich by possession and the poor by covetousness ; it sells the country to softness and vanity, and takes away from the State all its citizens, to make them slaves one to another, and one and all to public opinion.

It may be added that there is no government so subject to civil wars and intestine agitations as democratic or popular government, because there is none which has so strong and continual a tendency to change to another form, or which demands more vigilance and courage for its maintenance as it is. Under such a constitution above all, the citizen should arm himself with strength and constancy, and say, every day of his life, what a virtuous Count Palatine said in the Diet of Poland: Malo periculosam libertatem quam quietum servitium.

Were there a people of gods, their government would be democratic. So perfect a government is not for men.

There are three sorts of aristocracy – natural, elective and hereditary. The first is only for simple peoples; the third is the worst of all governments; the second is the best, and is aristocracy properly so called.

Besides the advantage that lies in the distinction between the two powers, it presents that of its members being chosen; for, in popular government, all the citizens are born magistrates; but here magistracy is confined to a few, who become such only by election. By this means uprightness, understanding, experience and all other claims to pre-eminence and public esteem become so many further guarantees of wise government.

In a word, it is the best and most natural arrangement that the wisest should govern the many, when it is assured that they will govern for its profit, and not for their own. There is no need to multiply instruments, or get twenty thousand men to do what a hundred picked men can do even better. But it must not be forgotten that corporate interest here begins to direct the public power less under the regulation of the general will, and that a further inevitable propensity takes away from the laws part of the executive power.

MONARCHY

So far, we have considered the prince as a moral and collective person, unified by the force of the laws, and the depositary in the State of the executive power. We have now to consider this power when it is gathered together into the hands of a natural person, a real man, who alone has the right to dispose of it in accordance with the laws. Such a person is called a monarch or king.

If no government is more vigorous than this, there is also none in which the particular will holds more sway and rules the rest more easily. Everything moves towards the same end indeed, but this end is by no means that of the public happiness, and even the force of the administration constantly shows itself prejudicial to the State.

Kings desire to be absolute, and men are always crying out to them from afar that the best means of being so is to get themselves loved by their people. This precept is all very well, and even in some respects very true. Unfortunately, it will always be derided at court. The power which comes of a people's love is no doubt the greatest ; but it is precarious and conditional, and princes will never rest content with it. The best kings desire to be in a position to be wicked, if they please, without forfeiting their mastery.

If it is hard for a great State to be well governed, it is much harder for it to be so by a single man; and everyone knows what happens when kings substitute others for themselves.

An essential and inevitable defect, which will always rank monarchical below republican government, is that in a republic the public voice hardly ever raises to the highest positions men who are not enlightened and capable, and such as to fill them with honour; while in monarchies those who rise to the top are most often merely petty blunderers, petty swindlers, and petty intriguers, whose petty talents cause them to get into the highest positions at Court, but, as soon as they have got there, serve only to make their ineptitude clear to the public.

Crowns have been made hereditary in certain families, and an order of succession has been set up, to prevent disputes from arising on the death of kings. That is to say, the disadvantages of regency have been put in place of those of election, apparent tranquillity has been preferred to wise administration, and men have chosen rather to risk having children, monstrosities, or imbeciles as rulers to having disputes over the choice of good kings.

Everything conspires to take away from a man who is set in authority over others the sense of justice and reason. Much trouble, we are told, is taken to teach young princes the art of reigning; but their education seems to do them no good. It would be better to begin by teaching them the art of obeying.

If royal education necessarily corrupts those who

receive it, what is to be hoped from a series of men brought up to reign? It is, then, wanton self-deception to confuse royal government with government by a good king. To see such government as it is in itself, we must consider it as it is under princes who are incompetent or wicked: for either they will come to the throne wicked or incompetent, or the throne will make them so.

Liberty, not being a fruit of all climates, is not within the reach of all peoples. The more this principle, laid down by Montesquieu, is considered, the more its truth is felt; the more it is combated, the more chance is given to confirm it by new proofs.

In fact, the more we reflect, the more we find the difference between free and monarchical States to be this: in the former, everything is used for the public advantage; in the aristocratic, the public forces and those of individuals are affected by each other, and either increases as the other grows weak; finally, instead of governing subjects to make them happy, despotism makes them wretched in order to govern them.

We find then, in every climate, natural causes according to which the form of government which it requires can be assigned, and we can even say what sort of inhabitants it should have.

As the particular will acts constantly in opposition to the general will, the government continually exerts itself against the Sovereignty. The greater this exertion becomes, the more the constitution changes; and, as there is in this case no other corporate will to create an equilibrium by resisting the will of the prince, sooner or later the prince must inevitably suppress the Sovereign and break the social treaty. This is the unavoidable and inherent defect which, from the very birth of the body politic, tends ceaselessly to destroy it, as age and death end by destroying the human body.

There are two general courses by which government degenerates : *i. e.* when it undergoes contraction, or when the State is dissolved.

Government undergoes contraction when it passes from the many to the few, that is, from democracy to aristocracy, and from aristocracy to royalty. To do so is its natural propensity.

When the State is dissolved, the abuse of government, whatever it is, bears the common name of *anarchy*. To distinguish, democracy degenerates into *ochlocracy*, and aristocracy into *oligarchy* ; and I would add that royalty degenerates into *tyranny* ; but this last word is ambiguous and needs explanation.

In vulgar usage, a tyrant is a king who governs violently and without regard for justice and law. In the exact sense, a tyrant is an individual who arrogates to himself the royal authority without having a right to it. *Tyrant* and *usurper* are thus perfectly synonymous terms.

Such is the natural and inevitable tendency of the best constituted governments. If Sparta and Rome perished, what State can hope to endure for ever ?

The body politic, as well as the human body, begins to die as soon as it is born, and carries in itself the causes of its destruction. But both may have a constitution that is more or less robust and suited to preserve them a longer or a shorter time. The constitution of man is the work of nature ; that of the State the work of art. It is not in men's power to prolong their own lives ; but it is for them to prolong as much as possible the life of the State, by giving it the best possible constitution. The best constituted State will have an end ; but it will end later than any other, unless some unforeseen accident brings about its untimely destruction.

The life-principle of the body politic lies in the sovereign authority. The legislative power is the heart of the State ; the executive power is its brain, which causes the movement of all the parts. The brain may become paralysed and the individual still live. A man may remain an imbecile and live ; but as soon as the heart ceases to perform its functions, the animal is dead.

The Sovereign, having no force other than the legislative power, acts only by means of the laws ; and the laws being solely the authentic acts of the general will, the Sovereign cannot act save when the people is assembled.

As soon as public service ceases to be the chief business of the citizens, and they would rather serve with their money than with their persons, the State is not far from its fall. When it is necessary to march out to war, they pay troops and stay at home : when it is necessary to meet in council, they name deputies and stay at home. By reason of idleness and money, they end by having soldiers to enslave their country and representatives to sell it.

The lukewarmness of patriotism, the activity of private interest, the vastness of States, conquest and the abuse of government suggested the method of having deputies or representatives of the people in the national assemblies. These are what, in some countries, men have presumed to call the Third Estate. Thus the individual interest of two orders is put first and second ; the public interest occupies only the third place.

Sovereignty, for the same reason as makes it inalienable, cannot be represented ; it lies essentially in the general will, and will does not admit of representation : it is either the same, or other ; there is no intermediate possibility. The deputies of the people, therefore, are not and cannot be its representatives : they are merely its stewards, and can carry through no definitive acts. Every law the people has not ratified in person is null and void – is, in fact, not a law. The moment a people allows itself to be represented, it is no longer free : it no longer exists.

The legislative power once well established, the next thing is to establish similarly the executive power. It has been held that this act of establishment was a contract between the people and the rulers it sets over itself. There is only one contract in the State, and that is the act of association, which in itself excludes the existence of a second.

The institution of government is not a contract, but a law ; the depositaries of the executive power are not the people's masters, but its officers ; it can set them up and pull them down when it likes ; for them there is no question of contract, but of obedience ; and in taking charge of the functions the State imposes on them they are doing no more than fulfilling their duty as citizens, without having the remotest right to argue about the conditions.

When therefore the people sets up an hereditary government, whether it be monarchical and confined to one family, or aristocratic and confined to a class, what it enters into is not an undertaking ; the administration is given a provisional form, until the people chooses to order it otherwise.

There is in the State no fundamental law that cannot be revoked, not excluding the social compact itself ; for if all the citizens assembled of one accord to break the compact, it is impossible to doubt that it would be very legitimately broken.

BOOK IV

There is but one law which, from its nature, needs unanimous consent. This is the social compact ; for civil association is the most voluntary of all acts. Every man being born free and his own master, no one, under any pretext whatsoever, can make any man subject without his consent.

If then there are opponents when the social compact is made, their opposition does not invalidate the contract, but merely prevents them from being included in it. They are foreigners among citizens. When the State is instituted, residence constitutes consent ; to dwell within its territory is to submit to the Sovereign.

Apart from this primitive contract, the vote of the majority always binds all the rest. This follows from the contract itself. The constant will of all the members of the State is the general will ; by virtue of it they are citizens and free. When in the popular assembly a law is proposed, what the people is asked is not exactly whether it approves or rejects the proposal, but whether it is in conformity with the general will, which is their will. Each man, in giving his vote, states his opinion on that point; and the general will is found by counting votes.

[*In the rest of Book IV, Rousseau examines the institutions of ancient Rome, as examples of the management of public affairs in a great Republic. Finally, he treats of the relation of religion with the State.*]

Religion, considered in relation to society, which is either general or particular, may also be divided into two kinds: the religion of man, and that of the citizen. The first, which has neither temples, nor altars, nor rites, and is confined to the purely internal cult of the supreme God and the eternal obligations of morality, is the religion of the Gospel pure and simple, the true theism, what may be called natural divine right or law. The other, which is codified in a single country, gives it its gods, its own tutelary patrons; it has its dogmas, its rites, and its external cult prescribed by law; outside the single nation that follows it, all the world is in its sight infidel, foreign and barbarous; the duties and rights of man extend for it only as far as its own altars. Of this kind were all the religions of early peoples, which we may define as civil or positive divine right or law.

There is a third sort of religion of a more singular kind, which gives men two codes of legislation, two rulers, and two countries, renders them subject to contradictory duties, and makes it impossible for them to be faithful both to religion and to citizenship. Such are the religions of the Lamas and of the Japanese, and such is Roman Christianity, which may be called the religion of the priest. It leads to a sort of mixed and anti-social code which has no name.

In their political aspect, all these three kinds of religion have their defects. The third is so clearly bad, that it is waste of time to stop to prove it such. All that destroys social unity is worthless ; all institutions that set man in contradiction to himself are worthless.

There remains the religion of man or Christianity – not the Christianity of today, but that of the Gospel, which is entirely different. By means of this holy, sublime, and real religion all men, being children of one God, recognise one another as brothers, and the society that unites them is not dissolved even at death.

But this religion, having no particular relation to the body politic, leaves the laws in possession of the force they have in themselves without making any addition to it ; and thus one of the great bonds that unite society considered in severalty fails to operate. Nay, more, so far from binding the hearts of the citizens to the State, it has the effect of taking them away from all earthly things. I know of nothing more contrary to the social spirit.

Christianity as a religion is entirely spiritual, occupied solely with heavenly things ; the country of the Christian is not of this world. He does his duty, indeed, but does it with profound indifference to the good or ill success of his cares. Provided he has nothing to reproach himself with, it matters little to him whether things go well or ill here on earth.

Christianity preaches only servitude and dependence. Its spirit is so favourable to tyranny that it always profits by such a *régime*. True Christians are made to be slaves, and they know it and do not much mind: this short life counts for too little in their eyes.

But let us come back to what is right, and settle our principles on this important point. The right which the social compact gives the Sovereign over the subjects does not, we have seen, exceed the limits of public expediency.* The subjects then owe the Sovereign an account of their opinions only to such an extent as they matter to the community. Now, it matters very much to the community that each citizen should have a religion. That will make him love his duty; but the dogmas of that religion concern the State and its members only so far as they have reference to morality and to the duties which he who professes them is bound to do to others. Each man may have, over and above, what opinions he pleases, without it being the Sovereign's business to take cognisance of them; for, as the Sovereign has no authority in the other world, whatever the lot of its subjects may be in the life to come, that is not its business, provided they are good citizens in this life.

* "In the republic," says the Marquis d'Argenson, "each man is perfectly free in what does not harm others." This is the invariable limitation, which it is impossible to define more exactly.

There is therefore a purely civil profession of faith of which the Sovereign should fix the articles, not exactly as religious dogmas, but as social sentiments without which a man cannot be a good citizen or a faithful subject. While it can compel no one to believe them, it can banish from the State whoever does not believe them – it can banish him, not for impiety, but as an anti-social being, incapable of truly loving the laws and justice, and of sacrificing, at need, his life to his duty. If anyone, after publicly recognising these dogmas, behaves as if he does not believe them, let him be punished by death: he has committed the worst of all crimes, that of lying before the law.

The dogmas of civil religion ought to be few, simple, and exactly worded, without explanation or commentary. The existence of a mighty, intelligent and beneficent Divinity, possessed of foresight and providence, the life to come, the happiness of the just, the punishment of the wicked, the sanctity of the social contract and the laws: these are its positive dogmas. Its negative dogmas I confine to one, intolerance, which is a part of the cults we have rejected.

Now that there is and can be no longer an exclusive national religion, tolerance should be given to all religions that tolerate others, so long as their dogmas contain nothing contrary to the duties of citizenship. But whoever dares to say: *Outside the Church is no salvation*, ought to be driven from the State.

EMILE

Rousseau had always showed a leaning toward the vocation of teacher. In 1735, when he was 23 years old, he wrote to his father that, of all the states he could consider, the only one for which he had "some predilection" was that of tutor to young men of rank. He made several trials of this occupation without too much success — at Lyon in 1740–1741, and in Paris in 1743. And as early as 1740 he had put his educational theories on paper in a "Plan" which foreshadowed certain characteristics of his Emile : *but at that time he had not undergone his moral reformation so antagonistic to the society of his day. During his stay at the Hermitage and at Montmorency, he passionately attacked the problem of education. Since civilisation appeared to him to have betrayed* "the natural man," *it was necessary that it be reconstructed : — a problem with which the Encyclopedists, his former friends, now his enemies, did not occupy themselves.*

"The literature and science of our day," *he wrote in his Preface,* "tend rather to destroy than to build up. We find fault after the manner of a master ; to suggest, we must adopt another style, a style less in accordance with the pride of the philosopher. In spite of all those books, whose only aim, so they say, is public utility, the most useful of all arts, the art of training men, is still neglected."

Rousseau worked on Emile *at the same time as on* The Social Contract. *The two works are related.*

The principles set forth in both are based on the essential liberty of natural man which should be safeguarded by education – and really assured by the lawmaker. Both are the boldest and most fruitful works to have come from Rousseau's pen, or to have been conceived by the pre-revolutionary spirit of the 18th century. Also, both of them were condemned to be burned, almost immediately after their appearance at the bookseller's. Emile, *finished in 1760, was published – and burned – in 1762.*

EMILE

OR EDUCATION

In the natural order men are all equal and their common calling is that of manhood, so that a well-educated man cannot fail to do well in that calling and those related to it. It matters little to me whether my pupil is intended for the army, the church, or the law. Before his parents chose a calling for him nature called him to be a man. Life is the trade I would teach him. The real object of our study is man and his environment.

Life is not breath, but action, the use of our senses, our mind, our faculties, every part of ourselves which makes us conscious of our being. Life consists less in length of days than in the keen sense of living.

Our wisdom is slavish prejudice, our customs consist in control, constraint, compulsion. Civilised man is born and dies a slave. The infant is bound up in swaddling clothes, the corpse is nailed down in his coffin. All his life long man is imprisoned by our institutions.

Fix your eyes on nature, follow the path traced by her. She keeps children at work, she hardens them by all kinds of difficulties, she soon teaches them the meaning of pain and grief. Accustom them therefore to the hardships they will have to face.

By slow and careful stages man and child learn to fear nothing.

All wickedness comes from weakness. The child is only naughty because he is weak; make him strong and he will be good; if we could do everything we should never do wrong. Of all the attributes of the Almighty, goodness is that which it would be hardest to dissociate from our conception of Him.

I shall not take pains to prevent Emile hurting himself; far from it, I should be vexed if he never hurt himself, if he grew up unacquainted with pain. To bear pain is his first and most useful lesson. Instead of keeping him mewed up in a stuffy room, take him out into a meadow every day; let him run about, let him struggle and fall again and again, the oftener the better; he will learn all the sooner to pick himself up.

What do you mean when you say, "Man is weak"? The term weak implies a relation, a relation of the creature to whom it is applied. An insect or a worm whose strength exceeds its needs is strong; an elephant, a lion, a conqueror, a hero, a god himself, whose needs exceed his strength is weak.

Oh, man! live your own life and you will no longer be wretched. Keep to your appointed place in the order of nature and nothing can tear you from it. Do not kick against the stern law of necessity.

That man is truly free who desires what he is able to perform, and does what he desires. This is my fundamental maxim. Apply it to childhood, and all the rules of education spring from it.

There are two kinds of dependence : dependence on things, which is the work of nature ; and dependence on men, which is the work of society. Dependence on things, being non-moral, does no injury to liberty and begets no vices ; dependence on men, being out of order, gives rise to every kind of vice, and through this master and slave become mutually depraved.

Keep the child dependent on things only. Let his wishes meet with physical obstacles only, or the punishment which results from his own actions, lessons which will be recalled when the same circumstances occur again. It is enough to prevent him from wrong doing without forbidding him to do wrong. Experience or lack of power should take the place of law.

Your child must not get what he asks, but what he needs ; he must never act from obedience, but from necessity.

The words *obey* and *command* will be excluded from his vocabulary, still more those of *duty* and *obligation* ; but the words strength, necessity, weakness, and constraint must have a large place in it.

Thus you will make him patient, equable, calm, and resigned, even when he does not get all he wants ; for it is in man's nature to bear patiently with the nature of things, but not with the ill-will of another.

Let us lay it down as an incontrovertible rule that the first impulses of nature are always right ; there is no original sin in the human heart ; the how and why of the entrance of every vice can be traced.

The education of the earliest years should be merely negative. It consists, not in teaching virtue or truth, but in preserving the heart from vice and from the spirit of error.

The only moral lesson which is suited for a child – the most important lesson for every time of life – is this : "Never hurt anybody." The very rule of well-doing, if not subordinated to this rule, is dangerous, false, and contradictory. Who is there who does no good ? Everyone does some good, the wicked as well as the righteous ; he makes one happy at the cost of the misery of a hundred, and hence spring all our misfortunes.

Human intelligence is finite, and not only can no man know everything, he cannot even acquire all the scanty knowledge of others. Since the contrary of every false proposition is a truth, there are as many truths as falsehoods. We must, therefore, choose what to teach. The small store which really contributes to our welfare alone deserves the study of a wise man, and therefore of a child whom one would have wise. He must know not merely what is, but what is useful.

Keep this truth ever before you – Ignorance never did anyone any harm, error alone is fatal, and we do not lose our way through ignorance but through self-confidence.

Let us transform our sensations into ideas, but do not let us jump all at once from the objects of sense to objects of thought. The latter are attained by means of the former. Let the senses be the only guide for the first workings of reason. No book but the world, no teaching but that of fact.

Teach your scholar to observe the phenomena of nature; if you would have it grow, do not be in too great a hurry to satisfy this curiosity. Let him know nothing because you have told him, but because he has learnt it for himself. If ever you substitute authority for reason he will cease to reason; he will be a mere plaything of other people's thoughts.

If he goes wrong let him alone, do not correct his mistakes; hold your tongue till he finds them out for himself and corrects them, or at most arrange something, as opportunity offers, which may show him his mistakes. If he never makes mistakes he will never learn anything thoroughly.

This is the essential point in my method – Do not teach the child many things, but never let him form inaccurate or confused ideas. I care not if he knows nothing provided he is not mistaken, and I only acquaint him with truths to guard him against the errors he might put in their place. Reason and judgment come slowly, prejudices flock to us in crowds, and from these he must be protected.

It is not your business to teach him the various sciences, but to give him a taste for them and methods of learning them when this taste is more mature. That is a fundamental principle of all good education.

The notions of things thus acquired for oneself are clearer and much more convincing than those acquired from the teaching of others; and not only is our reason not accustomed to a slavish submission to authority, but we develop greater ingenuity in discovering relations and connecting ideas.

Our real teachers are experience and emotion, and man will never learn what befits a man except under its own conditions.

As soon as we have contrived to give our pupil an idea of the word "Useful," we have got an additional means of controlling him.

"What is the use of that?" This is the sacred formula, the formula by which he and I test every action of our lives.

I do not like verbal explanations. Young people pay little heed to them, nor do they remember them. Things! Things! I cannot repeat it too often. We lay too much stress upon words; we teachers babble, and our scholars follow our example.

I hate books; they only teach us to talk about things we know nothing about. But since we must have books, there is one book which, to my thinking, supplies the best treatise on an education according to nature. What is this wonderful book? Is it Aristotle? Pliny? Buffon? No; it is *Robinson Crusoe*.

Your main object should be to keep out of your scholar's way all idea of such social relations as he cannot understand, but when the development of knowledge compels you to show him the mutual dependence of mankind, instead of showing him its moral side, turn all his attention at first towards industry and the mechanical arts which make men useful to one another.

The value set by the general public on the various arts is in inverse ratio to their real utility. They are even valued directly according to their uselessness.

What will become of your pupils if you let them acquire this foolish prejudice, if you share it yourself? If, for instance, they see you show more politeness in a jeweller's shop than in a locksmith's. What idea will they form of the true worth of the arts and the real value of things when they see, on the one hand, a fancy price and, on the other, the price of real utility, and that the more a thing costs the less it is worth? As soon as you let them get hold of these ideas, you may give up all attempt at further education; in spite of you they will be like all the other scholars – you have wasted fourteen years.

In everything the art which is most generally useful and necessary, is undoubtedly that which most deserves esteem.

Agriculture is the earliest and most honourable of arts; metal work I put next, then carpentry, and so on. This is the order in which the child will put them, if he has not been spoilt by vulgar prejudices. What valuable considerations Emile will derive from his Robinson in such matters.

Thus the idea of social relations is gradually developed in the child's mind, before he can really be an active member of human society. Emile sees that to get tools for his own use, other people must have theirs, and that he can get in exchange what he needs and they possess. I easily bring him to feel the need of such exchange and to take advantage of it.

Every man must live; this argument, which appeals to everyone with more or less force in proportion to his humanity, strikes me as unanswerable when applied to oneself.

If in this world there is any condition so miserable that one cannot live without wrong-doing, where the citizen is driven into evil, you should hang, not the criminal, but those who drove him into crime.

You reckon on the present order of society, without considering that this order is itself subject to inscrutable changes, and that you can neither foresee nor provide against the revolution which may affect your children. The great become small, the rich poor, the king a commoner. Does fate strike so seldom that you can count on immunity from her blows? The crisis is approaching, and we are on the edge of a revolution.

Outside the pale of society, the solitary, owing nothing to any man, may live as he pleases, but in society either he lives at the cost of others, or he owes them in labour the cost of his keep. Man in society is bound to work; rich or poor, weak or strong, every idler is a thief.

Stoop to the position of a working man, to rise above your own.

Emile shall learn a trade. "An honest trade, at least," you say. What do you mean by honest? Is not every useful trade honest? I would not make an embroiderer, a gilder, a polisher of him, like Locke's young gentleman. Neither would I make him a musician, an actor, or an author. I would rather have him a shoemaker than a poet, I would rather he paved streets than painted flowers on china. "But," you will say, "policemen, spies, and hangmen are useful people." There would be no use for them if it were not for the government.

Emile will not long be a workman before he discovers those social inequalities he had not previously observed.

We have made him a worker and a thinker ; we have now to make him loving and tender-hearted, to perfect reason through feeling. But before we enter on this new order of things, let us cast an eye over the stage we are leaving behind us, and perceive as clearly as we can how far we have got.

Emile knows little, but what he knows is really his own ; he has no half-knowledge. Among the few things he knows and knows thoroughly this is the most valuable, that there are many things he does not know now but may know some day, many more that other men know but he will never know, and an infinite number which nobody will ever know. He is large-minded, not through knowledge, but through the power of acquiring it ; he is open-minded, intelligent, ready for anything. I am content if he knows the "Wherefore" of his actions and the "Why" of his beliefs. For once more my object is not to supply him with exact knowledge, but the means of getting it when required, to teach him to value it at its true worth, and to love truth above all things.

Emile is industrious, temperate, patient, steadfast, and full of courage. His imagination is still asleep, so he has no exaggerated ideas of danger ; the few ills he feels he knows how to endure in patience, because he has not learnt to rebel against fate. As to death, he knows not what it means ; but accustomed as he is to submit without resistance to the law of necessity, he will die, if die he must, without a groan and without a struggle ; that is as much as we can demand of nature, in that hour which we all abhor. To live in freedom, and to be independent of human affairs, is the best way to learn how to die.

Do you think that the earlier years of a child, who has reached his fifteenth year in this condition, have been wasted ?

Our passions are the chief means of self-preservation ; to try to destroy them is therefore as absurd as it is useless ; this would be to overcome nature, to reshape God's handiwork.

I consider those who would prevent the birth of the passions almost as foolish as those who would destroy them.

But should we reason rightly, if from the fact that passions are natural to man, we inferred that all the passions we feel in ourselves and behold in others are natural ? All those which enslave and destroy us have another source ; nature does not bestow them on us ; we seize on them in her despite.

The people are mankind ; those who do not belong to the people are so few in number that they are not worth counting. Man is the same in every station of life ; if that be so, those ranks to which most men belong deserve most honour.

Society must be studied in the individual and the

individual in society; those who desire to treat politics and morals apart from one another will never understand either.

Since it is impossible in the state of nature that the difference between man and man should be great enough to make one dependent on another, there is in fact in this state of nature an actual and indestructible equality. In the civil state there is a vain and chimerical equality of right; the means intended for its maintenance, themselves serve to destroy it; and the power of the community, added to the power of the strongest for the oppression of the weak, disturbs the sort of equilibrium which nature has established between them. From this first contradiction spring all the other contradictions between the real and the apparent, which are to be found in the civil order. The many will always be sacrificed to the few, the common weal to private interest; those specious words – justice and subordination – will always serve as the tools of violence and the weapons of injustice.

I would have you so choose the company of a youth that he should think well of those among whom he lives, and I would have you so teach him to know the world that he should think ill of all that takes place in it. Let him know that man is by nature good, let him feel it, let him judge his neighbour by himself; but let him see how men are depraved and perverted by society; let him find the source of all their vices in their preconceived opinions.

Shall we make of Emile a knight-errant, a redresser of wrongs, a paladin? He will do all that he knows to be useful and good. He will do nothing more, and he knows that nothing is useful and good for him which is unbefitting his age. He knows that his first duty is to himself; that young men should distrust themselves; that they should act circumspectly; that they should show respect to those older than themselves, reticence and discretion in talking without cause, modesty in things indifferent, but courage in well doing, and boldness to speak the truth. Such were those illustrious Romans who, having been admitted into public life, spent their days in bringing criminals to justice and in protecting the innocent, without any motives beyond those of learning, and of the furtherance of justice and of the protection of right conduct.

Emile is not fond of noise or quarrelling, not only among men, but among animals. This peaceful spirit is one of the results of his education, which has never stimulated self-love or a high opinion of himself, and so has not encouraged him to seek his pleasure in domination and in the sufferings of others. The sight of suffering makes him suffer too; this is a natural feeling.

When I want to train a natural man, I do not want to make him a savage and to send him back to the woods, but that living in the whirl of social life it is enough that he should not let himself be carried away by the passions and prejudices of men; let him see with his eyes and feel with his heart, let him own no sway but that of reason.

I am aware that many of my readers will be surprised to find me tracing the course of my scholar through his early years without speaking to him of religion. At fifteen he will not even know that he has a soul, at eighteen even he may not be ready to learn about it. For if he learns about it too soon, there is the risk of his never really knowing anything about it.

"We must believe in God if we would be saved." This doctrine wrongly understood is the root of bloodthirsty intolerance and the cause of all the futile teaching which strikes a deadly blow at human reason by training it to cheat itself with mere words.

The obligation of faith assumes the possibility of belief.

There are circumstances in which one can be saved without belief in God, and these circumstances occur in the case of children or madmen when the human mind is incapable of the operations necessary to perceive the Godhead. From the same principle it is plain that any man having reached old age without faith in God will not, therefore, be deprived of God's presence in another life if his blindness was not wilful ; and I maintain that it is not always wilful.

Let us beware of proclaiming the truth to those who cannot as yet comprehend it, for to do so is to try to inculcate error. It would be better to have no idea at all of the Divinity than to have mean, grotesque, harmful, and unworthy ideas ; to fail to perceive the Divine is a lesser evil than to insult it.

The neglect of all religion soon leads to the neglect of man's duty.

PROFESSION OF FAITH OF A SAVOYARD VICAR

The Profession of Faith of a Savoyard Vicar *which is suddenly interpolated into Book IV of* Emile *is like a different work altogether. In its amplitude and fervour, these pages form the great illumination in the life of Rousseau and in philosophical and religious thought in the 18th century.*

Later telling of "the great revolution" *which came about in him following the thunderbolt in* 1749 – *when* "another moral world unveiled itself to my gaze," *and he felt himself* "obliged to undertake this great review of his thought" – *Rousseau spoke of the repulsion which came over him with regard to the Encyclopedists, his contemporaries* – "ardent missionaries of Atheism, and very imperious dogmatists, they did not endure without anger that on any point there might exist anyone who dared to think otherwise than they. . ." "Never," *he affirmed*, "did I adopt their desolating doctrine; and this resistance to men so intolerant, who moreover had their own views, was not one of the least causes for attracting their animosity." – *He undertook to formulate his own philosophy. This was a difficult labour, and he was often on the verge of giving it up. Nevertheless he persisted.* "For the first time in my life I had courage." *To him it was a question of the* "eternal fate of his soul."

"The result of my painful researches was practically

that which I gave out in the *Profession of Faith of the Savoyard Vicar*, a work unworthily prostituted and profaned in the present generation, but which some day may make a revolution among men, if ever good sense and good faith are born again among them." (*Third* Reverie of a Solitary Stroller *written in* 1777, *on the eve of his death.*)

It is indeed true that this little work, so vast in scope, – which aroused the anger of both Catholics and Protestants and led to the author's persecution by both – had incalculable reverberations in the heart of the generation that followed his.

PROFESSION OF FAITH OF A SAVOYARD VICAR

I cannot understand how anyone can be a sceptic sincerely and on principle. Either such philosophers do not exist or they are the most miserable of men. Doubt with regard to what we ought to know is a condition too violent for the human mind ; it cannot long be endured ; in spite of itself the mind decides one way or another, and it prefers to be deceived rather than to believe nothing.

I consulted the philosophers, I examined their various theories ; I found them all alike proud, assertive, dogmatic, professing, even in their so-called scepticism, to know everything, proving nothing, scoffing at each other. Weigh their arguments, they are all destructive ; they are only agreed in arguing with each other. I could find no way out of my uncertainty by listening to them.

I suppose this prodigious diversity of opinion is caused, in the first place, by the weakness of the human intellect ; and, in the second, by pride. We have no means of measuring this vast machine, we are unable to calculate its workings ; we know neither its guiding principles nor its final purpose ; we do not know ourselves, we know neither our nature nor the spirit that moves us ; we scarcely know whether man is one or many ; we are surrounded by impenetrable mysteries. These mysteries are beyond the region of sense, we think we can penetrate them by the light of reason, but we fall back on our imagination. Through this imagined world each forces a way for himself which he holds to be right; none can tell whether his path will lead him to the goal. Yet we long to know and understand it all. A fragment of some vast whole whose bounds are beyond our gaze, a fragment abandoned by its Creator to our foolish quarrels, we are vain enough to want to determine the nature of that whole and our own relations with regard to it.

The first thing I learned from these considerations was to restrict my enquiries to what directly concerned myself, to rest in profound ignorance of everything else, and not even to trouble myself to doubt anything beyond what I required to know.

I also realised that the philosophers, far from ridding me of my vain doubts, only multiplied the doubts that tormented me and failed to remove any one of them. So I chose another guide and said, "Let me follow the Inner Light; it will not lead me so far astray as others have done, or if it does it will be my own fault, and I shall not go so far wrong if I follow my own illusions as if I trusted to their deceits."

I exist, and I have senses through which I receive impressions. This is the first truth that strikes me and I am forced to accept it. Not only do I exist, but other entities exist also, that is to say, the objects of my sensations; and even if these objects are merely ideas, still these ideas are not me.

Everything outside myself, everything which acts upon my senses, I call matter, and all the particles of matter which I suppose to be united into separate entities I call bodies. Thus all the disputes of the idealists and the realists have no meaning for me;

their distinctions between the appearance and the reality of bodies are wholly fanciful.

I am now as convinced of the existence of the universe as of my own. I next consider the objects of my sensations, and I find that I have the power of comparing them, so I perceive that I am endowed with an active force of which I was not previously aware.

There is not a being in the universe which may not be regarded as in some respects the common centre of all, around which they are grouped, so that they are all reciprocally end and means in relation to each other. The mind is confused and lost amid these innumerable relations, not one of which is itself confused or lost in the crowd. What absurd assumptions are required to deduce all this harmony from the blind mechanism of matter set in motion by chance!

I believe that the world is governed by a wise and powerful will; I see it or rather I feel it, and it is a great thing to know this. But has this same world always existed, or has it been created? Is there one source of all things? Are there two or many? What is their nature? I know not; and what concern is it of mine?

Whether matter is eternal or created, whether its origin is passive or not, it is still certain that the whole is one, and that it proclaims a single intelligence; for I see nothing that is not part of the same ordered system, nothing which does not cooperate to the same end, namely, the conservation of all within the established order. This being who wills and can perform his will, this being active through his own power, this being, whoever he may be, who moves the universe and orders all things, is what I call God. To this name I add the ideas of intelligence, power, will, which I have brought together, and that of kindness which is their necessary consequence; but for all this I know no more of the being to which I ascribe them. He hides himself alike from my senses and my understanding; the more I think of him, the more perplexed I am; I know full well that he exists, and that he exists of himself alone; I know that my existence depends on his, and that everything I know depends upon him also. I see God everywhere in his works; I feel him within myself; I behold him all around me; but if I try to ponder him himself, if I try to find out where he is, what he is, what is his substance, he escapes me and my troubled spirit finds nothing.

Convinced of my unfitness, I shall never argue about the nature of God unless I am driven to it by the feeling of his relations with myself. But when, in my desire to discover my own place within my species, I consider its different ranks and the men who fill them, where am I now? What a sight meets my eyes! Where is now the order I perceived? Nature showed me a scene of harmony and proportion; the human race shows me nothing but confusion and disorder. The elements agree together; men are in a state of chaos. I behold the earth, and there is evil upon it.

Man is free to act, and as such he is animated by an immaterial substance; that is the third article of my creed.

If man is at once active and free, he acts of his own accord; what he does freely is no part of the system marked out by Providence and it cannot be imputed to Providence. Providence does not will the evil that man does when he misuses the freedom given to him ; neither does Providence prevent him doing it, either because the wrong done by so feeble a creature is as nothing in its eyes, or because it could not prevent it without doing a greater wrong and degrading his nature. Providence has made him free that he may choose the good and refuse the evil. It has made him capable of this choice if he uses rightly the faculties bestowed upon him, but it has so strictly limited his powers that the misuse of his freedom cannot disturb the general order. The evil that man does reacts upon himself without affecting the system of the world.

It is the abuse of our powers that makes us unhappy and wicked. Our cares, our sorrows, our sufferings are of our own making. Moral ills are undoubtedly the work of man, and physical ills would be nothing but for our vices which have made us liable to them. Death is the cure for the evils you bring upon yourself ; nature would not have you suffer perpetually.

O Man ! seek no further for the author of evil ; thou art he. There is no evil but the evil you do or the evil you suffer, and both come from yourself. Evil in general can only spring from disorder, and in the order of the world I find a never-failing system.

Where all is well, there is no such thing as injustice. Justice and goodness are inseparable ; now goodness is the necessary result of boundless power and of that self-love which is innate in all sentient beings. The omnipotent projects himself, so to speak, into the being of his creatures. Creation and preservation are the everlasting work of power; it does not act on that which has no existence; God is not the God of the dead; he could not harm and destroy without injury to himself. The omnipotent can only will what is good. Therefore he who is supremely good, because he is supremely powerful, must also be supremely just, otherwise he would contradict himself; for that love of order which creates order we call goodness and that love of order which preserves order we call justice.

If the soul is immaterial, it may survive the body; and if it so survives, Providence is justified. Had I no other proof of the immaterial nature of the soul, the triumph of the wicked and the oppression of the righteous in this world would be enough to convince me. I should seek to resolve so appalling a discord in the universal harmony. I should say to myself, "All is not over with life, everything finds its place at death." I should still have to answer the question, "What becomes of man when all we know of him through our senses has vanished?" This question no longer presents any difficulty to me when I admit the two substances. When the union of soul and body is destroyed, I think one may be dissolved and the other may be preserved. Why should the destruction of the one imply the destruction of the other? On the contrary, so unlike in their nature, they were during their union in a highly unstable condition, and when this union comes to an end they both return to their natural state; the active vital substance regains all the force which it expended to set in motion the passive dead substance. Alas ! my vices make me only too well aware that man is but half alive during this life ; the life of the soul only begins with the death of the body.

But what is that life ? Is the soul of man in its nature immortal ? I know not. My finite understanding cannot hold the infinite ; what is called eternity eludes my grasp. What can I assert or deny, how can I reason with regard to what I cannot conceive ? I believe that the soul survives the body for the maintenance of order ; who knows if this is enough to make it eternal ? However, I know that the body is worn out and destroyed by the division of its parts, but I cannot conceive a similar destruction of the conscious nature, and as I cannot imagine how it can die, I presume that it does not die. As this assumption is consoling and in itself not unreasonable, why should I fear to accept it ?

Do not ask me whether the torments of the wicked will endure for ever, whether the goodness of their creator can condemn them to the eternal suffering. All the same I find it hard to believe that they will be condemned to everlasting torments. If the supreme justice calls for vengeance, it claims it in this life.

Thus it is that, in the contemplation of God in his works, and in the study of such of his attributes as it concerned me to know, I have slowly grasped and developed the idea, at first partial and imperfect, which I have formed of this Infinite Being. When I hear it said that my soul is spiritual and that God is a spirit, I revolt against this abasement of the divine essence ; as if God and my soul were of one and the same nature ! As if God were not the one and only absolute being, the only really active, feeling, thinking, willing being, from whom we derive our thought, feeling, motion, will, our freedom and our very existence ! We are free because he wills our freedom, and his inexplicable substance is to our souls what our souls are to our bodies.

The more I strive to envisage his infinite essence the less do I comprehend it ; but it is, and that is enough for me ; the less I understand, the more I adore. I abase myself, saying, "Being of beings, I am because thou art ; to fix my thoughts on thee is to ascend to the source of my being. The best use I can make of my reason is to resign it before thee ; my mind delights, my weakness rejoices, to feel myself overwhelmed by thy greatness."

Having thus deduced from the perception of objects of sense and from my inner consciousness, which leads me to judge of causes by my native reason, the principal truths which I require to know, I must now seek such principles of conduct as I can draw from them, and such rules as I must lay down for my guidance in the fulfilment of my destiny in this world, according to the purpose of my Maker. Still following the same method, I do not derive these rules from the principles of the higher philosophy, I find them in the depths of my heart, traced by nature in characters which nothing can efface. I need only consult myself with regard to what I wish to do ; what I feel to be right is right, what I feel to be wrong is wrong ; conscience is the best casuist; and it is only when we haggle with conscience that we have recourse to the subtleties of argument.

There is therefore at the bottom of our hearts an innate principle of justice and virtue, by which, in spite of our maxims, we judge our own actions or those of others to be good or evil; and it is this principle that I call conscience.

But it is not enough to be aware that there is such a guide; we must know her and follow her. If she speaks to all hearts, how is it that so few give heed to her voice? She speaks to us in the language of nature, and everything leads us to forget that tongue.

There is an age when the heart is eager, unquiet, greedy of a happiness which is still unknown, a happiness which it seeks, and, deceived by the senses, it settles at length upon the empty show of happiness and thinks it has found it where it is not. These illusions, if they lead me astray, I am at least no longer deceived by them; I know them for what they are, and even when I give way to them, I despise myself; far from regarding them as the goal of my happiness, I behold in them an obstacle to it. I long for the time when, freed from the fetters of the body, I shall be myself, at one with myself, no longer torn in two, when I myself shall suffice for my own happiness. Meanwhile I am happy even in this life, for I make small account of all its evils, in which I regard myself as having little or no part, while all the real good that I can get out of this life depends on myself alone.

To raise myself so far as may be even now to this state of happiness, strength, and freedom, I exercise myself in lofty contemplation. I consider the order of the universe, not to explain it by any futile system, but to revere it without ceasing, to adore the wise Author who reveals himself in it. I hold intercourse with him; I immerse all my powers in his divine essence; I am overwhelmed by his kindness, I bless him and his gifts, but I do not pray to him. What should I ask of him – to change the order of nature, to work miracles on my behalf? Should I, who am bound to love above all things the order which he has established in his wisdom and maintained by his providence, should I desire the disturbance of that order on my own account? No, that rash prayer would deserve to be punished rather than to be granted.

In my well-founded self-distrust the only thing that I ask of God, or rather expect from his justice, is to correct my error if I go astray, if that error is dangerous to me. To be honest I need not think myself infallible; my opinions, which seem to me true, may be so many lies; for what man is there who does not cling to his own beliefs; and how many men are agreed in everything? The illusion which deceives me may indeed have its source in myself, but it is God alone who can remove it. I have done all I can to attain to truth; but its source is beyond my reach.

In my exposition you find nothing but natural religion; strange that we should need more!

Do not let us confuse the outward forms of religion with religion itself. The service God requires is of the heart; and when the heart is sincere that is ever the same.

God desires to be worshipped in spirit and in truth ; this duty belongs to every religion, every country, every individual. As to the form of worship, if order demands uniformity, that is only a matter of discipline and needs no revelation.

Let us therefore seek honestly after truth ; let us yield nothing to the claims of birth, to the authority of parents and pastors, but let us summon to the bar of conscience and of reason all that they have taught us from our childhood. In vain do they exclaim, "Submit your reason ;" a deceiver might say as much ; I must have reasons for submitting my reason.

Faith is confirmed and strengthened by understanding ; the best religion is of necessity the simplest. He who hides beneath mysteries and contradictions the religion that he preaches to me, teaches me at the same time to distrust that religion. The God whom I adore is not the God of darkness, he has not given me understanding in order to forbid me to use it ; to tell me to submit my reason is to insult the giver of reason. The minister of truth does not tyrannise over my reason, he enlightens it.

We have three principal forms of religion in Europe. One accepts one revelation, another two, and another three. Each hates the others, showers curses on them, accuses them of blindness, obstinacy, hardness of heart, and falsehood.

In all three revelations the sacred books are written in languages unknown to the people who believe in them.

I can never believe that every man is obliged to know what is contained in books, and that he who is out of reach of these books, and of those who understand them, will be punished for an ignorance which is no fault of his. Were not all these books written by men? Why then should a man need them to teach him his duty, and how did he learn his duty before these books were in existence? Either he must have learnt his duties for himself, or his ignorance must have been excused.

Two thirds of mankind are neither Jews, Mahometans, nor Christians; and how many millions of men have never heard the name of Moses, Jesus Christ, or Mahomet?

I regard all individual religions as so many wholesome institutions which prescribe a uniform method by which each country may do honour to God in public worship; institutions which may each have its reason in the country, the government, the genius of the people, or in other local causes which make one preferable to another in a given time or place. I think them all good alike, when God is served in a fitting manner. True worship is of the heart. God rejects no homage, however offered, provided it is sincere.

While we await further knowledge, let us respect public order; in every country let us respect the laws, let us not disturb the form of worship prescribed by law; let us not lead its citizens into disobedience; for we have no certain knowledge that it is good for them to abandon their own opinions for others, and on the other hand we are quite certain that it is a bad thing to disobey the law.

Whatever decision you come to, remember that the real duties of religion are independent of human institutions; that a righteous heart is the true temple of the Godhead ; that in every land, in every sect, to love God above all things and to love our neighbour as ourself is the whole law ; remember there is no religion which absolves us from our moral duties ; that these alone are really essential, that the service of the heart is the first of these duties, and that without faith there is no such thing as true virtue.

Shun those who, under the pretence of explaining nature, sow destructive doctrines in the heart of men, those whose apparent scepticism is a hundredfold more self-assertive and dogmatic than the firm tone of their opponents. Under the arrogant claim, that they alone are enlightened, true, honest, they subject us imperiously to their far-reaching decisions, and profess to give us, as the true principles of all things, the unintelligible systems framed by their imagination. Moreover, they overthrow, destroy, and trample under foot all that men reverence ; they rob the afflicted of their last consolation in their misery ; they deprive the rich and powerful of the sole bridle of their passions ; they tear from the very depths of man's heart all remorse for crime, and all hope of virtue ; and they boast, moreover, that they are the benefactors of the human race. Truth, they say, can never do a man harm. I think so too, and to my mind that is strong evidence that what they teach is not true.*

* Bayle has proved very satisfactorily that fanaticism is more harmful than atheism, and that cannot be denied ; but what he has not taken the trouble to say, though it is none the less true, is this : Fanaticism, though cruel and bloodthirsty, is still a great and powerful passion, which stirs the heart of man, teaching him to despise death, and giving him an enormous motive power, which only needs to be guided rightly to produce the noblest virtues ; while irreligion, and the argumentative philo-

Be honest and humble; learn how to be ignorant, then you will never deceive yourself or others. If ever your talents are so far cultivated as to enable you to speak to other men, always speak according to your conscience, without caring for their applause. The abuse of knowledge causes incredulity. The learned always despise the opinions of the crowd; each of them must have his own opinion. A haughty philosophy leads to atheism just as blind devotion leads to fanaticism. Avoid these extremes; keep steadfastly to the path of truth, or what seems to you truth, in simplicity of heart, and never let yourself be turned aside by pride or weakness. Dare to confess God before the philosophers; dare to preach humanity to the intolerant. It may be you will stand alone, but you will bear within you a witness which will make the witness of men of no account with you. Let them love or hate, let them read your writings or despise them;

---

sophic spirit generally, on the other hand, assaults the life and enfeebles it, degrades the soul, concentrates all the passions in the basest self-interest, in the meanness of the human self; thus it saps unnoticed the very foundations of all society; for what is common to all these private interests is so small that it will never outweigh their opposing interests.

If atheism does not lead to bloodshed, it is less from love of peace than from indifference to what is good; as if it mattered little what happened to others, provided the sage remained undisturbed in his study. His principles do not kill men, but they prevent their birth, by destroying the morals by which they were multiplied, by detaching them from their fellows, by reducing all their affections to a secret selfishness, as fatal to population as to virtue. The indifference of the philosopher is like the peace in a despotic state; it is the repose of death; war itself is not more destructive.

Thus fanaticism, though its immediate results are more fatal than those of what is now called the philosophic mind, is much less fatal in its after effects.

no matter. Speak the truth and do the right; the one thing that really matters is to do one's duty in this world; and when we forget ourselves we are really working for ourselves.

JULIE

OR THE NEW HÉLOÏSE

Rousseau had fled from Paris in April 1756. *He took up his abode in the country, in the little house of the Hermitage, on the edge of the forest of Montmorency. It was spring, and Rousseau lived in his dreams.* "Devoured by a need of loving, which he had never been able to satisfy, he saw himself on the verge of old age and death without ever really having lived," *Rousseau took pity on himself and indulged his melancholy. His imagination peopled his loneliness with charming beings of his own creation. He imagined to himself* "the love, the friendship, the two idols of his heart under the most delightful aspect. . ." *He imagined two friends* "of similar character, but different . . . not perfect but to his taste, lovingly generous and full of sensibility." "I made one dark and the other fair," *he said*, "one lively and the other gentle, one wise and the other weak, but of a weakness so touching it almost became virtue. To one of the two I gave a lover who was the dear friend of the other, and even something more; but I allowed no rivalry, no quarrels, no jealousy, because I wished to spoil nothing of this cheerful picture by anything that degraded nature. Under the sway of my two charming models, I identified myself with the lover and friend; but I made him young and lovable, giving him moreover the virtues and defects which I felt I possessed. – In order to place my personages in a setting suitable to them, I passed over in my mind the most beautiful spots I had seen in my travels. For a long time I thought of the Barromean Islands, whose delightful aspect had transported me; but I found there too much of ornament and art for my personages. Nevertheless I had to have a lake, and I ended by choosing that one around which my heart has never ceased to roam. I decided on the part of this lake (Léman) where I have long fixed my residence in that imaginary happiness to which I have been restricted by my fate. I established my young wards at Vevey. . . I first jotted down upon paper several scanty letters. . . The first two parts of the book were written almost entirely in this manner, without my having any well-formed plan. . . After much effort, powerless to rid myself of all these imaginings, I delivered myself over entirely to them, and occupied myself in trying to put enough order and continuity in my story to make a novel. . ." (*Confessions, Book IX.*)

JULIE

OR THE NEW HÉLOÏSE

I am of opinion, when once the understanding is a little developed by reflection, it is better to reason for ourselves than to depend upon books for the discovery of truth; for by that means it will make a much stronger impression; whilst on the contrary, by taking things for granted, we view objects by halves and in a borrowed light. We are richer than we think; yet, says Montaigne, our whole education consists in borrowing. We are taught rather to use the wealth of other men, than break into our own store.

The grand error of young students is a too implicit dependence upon books, and too much diffidence in their own capacity; without reflecting that they are much less liable to be misled by their own reason, than by the sophistry of systematical writers. If we would but consult our own feelings, we should easily distinguish virtue and beauty: we do not want to be taught either of these; but examples of extreme virtue and superlative beauty are less common, and these are therefore more difficult to be understood. Our vanity leads us to mistake our own peculiar imbecility for that of nature and to think those qualities chimerical which we do not perceive within ourselves; idleness and vice rest upon pretended impossibility, and men of little genius conclude that things which are uncommon have no existence. These errors we must endeavour to eradicate, and by using ourselves to contemplate grand objects, destroy the notion of their impossibility. Thus, by degrees, our emulation is roused by example, our taste refines, and everything indifferent becomes intolerable.

But let us not have recourse to books for principles which may be found within ourselves. What have we to do with the idle disputes of philosophers concerning virtue and happiness? Let us rather employ that time in being virtuous and happy, which others waste in fruitless enquiries after the means: let us rather imitate great examples, than busy ourselves with systems and opinions.

I always believed that virtue was in reality active beauty; or at least that they were intimately connected, and sprung from the same source in nature. From this idea it follows that wisdom and taste are to be improved by the same means, and that a mind truly sensible of the charms of virtue must receive an equal impression from every other kind of beauty. Yet accurate and refined perception are to be acquired only by habit; and hence it is that we see a painter, in viewing a fine prospect or a good picture, in raptures at certain objects, which a common observer would not even have seen. How many real impressions do we perceive, which we cannot account for? how many *je-ne-sais-quoi* frequently occur, which taste only can determine? Taste is, in some degree, the microscope of judgement; it brings small objects to our view, and its operations begin where those of judgement end. How then shall we proceed in its cultivation? By exercising our sight as well as feeling, and by judgement of the beautiful from inspection, as we judge of virtue from sensation.

In what is called honour, there is a material distinction between that which is founded on the opinion of the world, and that which is derived from self-esteem. The first is nothing but the loud voice of foolish prejudice, which has no more stability than the wind ; but the basis of the latter is fixed in the eternal truth of morality. The honour of the world may be of advantage with regard to fortune ; but as it cannot reach the soul, it has no influence on real happiness. True honour, on the contrary, is the very essence of felicity ; for it is that alone inspires the permanent interior satisfaction which constitutes the happiness of a rational being.

What wretch dares preach that virtue which he will not practice ? Whosoever suffers himself to be thus blinded by his passions, will soon find himself punished in a loathing for those very sensations to which he sacrificed his honour. There can be no pleasure in any enjoyment which the heart cannot approve, and which tends to sink in our estimation the object of our love. Abstract the idea of perfection and our enthusiasm vanishes ; take away our esteem, and love is at an end. How is it possible for a woman to honour a man who dishonours himself ? and how can he adore the person who was weak enough to abandon herself to a vile seducer ? Mutual contempt therefore is the consequence ; their very passions will grow burdensome, and they will have lost their honour without finding happiness.

Ah, Julie, too much sensibility, too much tenderness, proves the bitterest curse instead of the most fruitful blessing : vexation and disappointment are its certain consequences. The temperature of the air, the change of the seasons, the brilliancy of the sun, or thickness of the fogs, are so many moving springs to the unhappy possessor, and he becomes the wanton sport of their arbitration : his thoughts, his satisfaction, his happiness depend on the blowing of the winds. Swayed as he is by prejudices, and distracted by passions, the sentiments of his heart find continual opposition from the axioms of his head. Should he perchance square his conduct to the undeviable rule of right, and set up truth for his standard, instead of profit and convenience, he is sure to fall a martyr to the maxims of his integrity ; the world will join in the cry, and hunt him down as a common enemy. He will search for supreme happiness, without taking into account the infirmities of his nature ; thus his affections and his reason will be engaged in a perpetual warfare, and unbounded ideas and desires must pave the way for endless disappointments.

Forbear then giving way to a self-disesteem more dangerous and destructive than any weakness of which you could be guilty. Does true love debase the soul ? No : nor can any crime, which is the result of that love, ever rob you of that enthusiastic ardour for truth and honour, which so raised you above yourself.

True love is the chastest of all human connexions ; and the sacred flame of love should purify our natural inclinations by concentring them in one object. It is love that secures us from temptation, and makes the whole sex indifferent, except the beloved individual. To a woman indifferent to love, every man is the same, and all are men ; but to her whose heart is truly susceptible of that refined passion, there is no other man in the world but her lover. What do I say? Is a lover no more than a man? He is a being far superior! There exists not a man in the creation with her who truly loves: her lover is more, and all others are less; they live for each other, and are the only beings of their species. They have no desires; they love. The heart is not led by, but leads the senses, and throws over their errors the veil of delight. There is nothing obscene but in lewdness and its gross language. Real love, always modest, seizes not impudently its favours, but steals them with timidity. Its flame purifies all caresses.

Can we be deprived of virtues we really possess by false aspersions of calumny? Do the insults of a drunken man prove such insults deserved? Or does the honour of the virtuous and prudent lie at the mercy of the first brute he meets? Will you tell me that fighting a duel shews a man to have courage, and that this is sufficient to efface the dishonour, and prevent the reproach, due to all other vices? I would ask you, what kind of honour can dictate such a decision? Or what arguments justify it? On such principles a knave needs only fight to cease to be a knave; the assertions of a liar become true when they are maintained at the point of the sword; and, if you were even accused of killing a man, you have only to kill a second, to prove the accusation false. Thus virtue, vice, honour, infamy, truth, and falsehood all derive their existence from the event of a duel. There is no other law than violence, no other argument than murder: all the reparation due to the insulted, is to kill them, and every offense is equally washed away by the blood of the offender or the offended. If wolves themselves could reason, would they entertain maxims more inhuman than these?

Beware then of confounding the sacred name of honour with that barbarous prejudice, which subjects every virtue to the decision of the sword, and is only adapted to make men daring villains. Do you not see that the crimes, which shame and a sense of honour have not prevented, are screened and multiplied by a false shame and the fear of reproach? It is this fear which makes men hypocrites and liars: it is this which makes them imbrue their hands in the blood of their friends, for an indiscreet word, which should have been forgotten, for a merited reproach too severe to be borne. It is this which transforms the abused and fearful maid into an infernal fury.

Do you know any crime equal to wilful murder? If humanity also be the basis of every virtue, what must be thought of the man, whose blood-thirsty and depraved disposition prompts him to seek the life of his fellow-creature?

What though it be true, that a man is despised who refuses to fight; which contempt is most to be feared, that of others for doing well, or that of ourselves for having acted ill? He who has a proper esteem for himself is little sensible to the unjust reproach cast on him by others, and is only afraid of deserving it. Probity and virtue depend not on the opinion of the world, but on the nature of things; and though all mankind should approve of the action you are about, it would not be the less shameful in itself. But it is a false notion, that to refrain from it, through a virtuous motive, would be bringing yourself into contempt. The virtuous man, whose whole life is irreproachable, and who never betrayed any marks of cowardice, will refuse to stain his hands with blood, and will be only the more respected for such refusal. Always ready to serve his country, to protect the weak, to discharge his duty on the most dangerous occasions, and to defend in every just and reasonable cause whatever is dear to him, at the hazard of his life, he displays throughout the whole of his conduct that unshaken fortitude, which is inseparable from true courage. Animated by the testimony of a good conscience, he appears undaunted, and neither flies from, nor seeks, his enemy. It is easily observed that he fears less to die than to act basely ; that he dreads the crime, but not the danger. If at any time the mean prejudices of the world raise a clamour against him, the conduct of his whole life is his testimony, and every action is approved by a behaviour so uniformly irreproachable.

I would have courage exerted only on lawful occasions, and not an idle parade made of it when it is unnecessary, as if there was some fear of not having it ready when it should be called for. There are cowards who will make one effort to exert their courage, that they may have a pretense to avoid danger the rest of their lives. True courage is more constant and less impetuous ; it is always what it ought to be, and wants neither the spur nor the rein ; the man of real magnanimity carries it always about him ; in fighting he exerts it against his enemy ; in company against backbiting and falsehood, and on a sick bed against the attacks of pain and the horrors of death. That fortitude of mind which inspires true courage is always exerted ; it places virtue out of the reach of events, and does not consist in braving danger, but in not fearing it.

All other pretenses to bravery are wild, extravagant, and brutal ; it is even cowardice to submit to them ; and I despise as much the man who runs himself into needless danger, as him who turns his back on what he ought to encounter.

All this, added to my natural aversion to cruelty, fills me with such horror at duels, that I regard them as instances of the lowest degree of brutality into which mankind can possibly descend. I look upon those who go cheerfully to a duel, in no other light than as wild beasts going to tear each other to pieces ; and if there remain the least sentiments of humanity within them, I think the murdered less to be pitied than the murderer.

How many great families would sink again into oblivion, if we respected only those which descended from truly respectable originals ? Judge of the past by the present : for two or three honest citizens ennobled by virtuous means, a thousand knaves find every day the way to aggrandize themselves and families. But to what end serves that nobility, of which their descendants are so proud unless it be to prove the injustice and infamy of their ancestors ? There are, I must confess, a great number of bad men among the common people ; but the odds are always twenty to one against a gentleman, that he is descended from a rascal.

In what consists the honour, then, of that nobility of which you are so tenacious ? How does it affect the glory of one's country or the good of mankind ? A mortal enemy to liberty and the laws, what did it ever produce in most of those countries where it has flourished, but the rod of tyranny and the oppression of the people ?

Justice and the fitness of things require that everyone should be disposed of in a manner the most advantageous to himself and to society. These two amiable minds were doubtless formed by the hands of nature for each other. In a peaceful and happy union, at liberty to exert their talents and display their virtues, they might have enlightened the world with the splendour of their examples. Why should an absurd prejudice, then, cross the eternal directions of nature, and subvert the harmony of thinking Beings ? Why should the vanity of a cruel father thus hide their light under a bushel, and wound those tender and benevolent hearts, which were formed to soothe the pangs of others ? Are not the ties of marriage the most free, as well as the most sacred of all engagements ? Yes, every law to lay a constraint on them is unjust. Every father, who presumes to form or break them, is a tyrant. This chaste and holy tie of nature is neither subjected to sovereign power nor paternal authority ; but to the authority only of that common parent who hath the power over our hearts, and, by commanding their union, can at the same time make them love each other.

To what end are natural conveniences sacrificed to those of opinion ? A disagreement in rank and fortune loses itself in marriage, nor doth any equality therein tend to make the marriage state happy ; but a disagreement in person and disposition ever remains, and is that which makes it necessarily miserable. A child that hath no rule of conduct but her fond passion, will frequently make a bad choice ; but the father who has no other rule for his than the opinion of the world, will make a worse. A daughter may want knowledge and experience to form a proper judgment of the discretion and conduct of men ; a good father ought doubtless in that case to advise her. He has a right, it is even his duty to say, "My child, this is a man of probity, or that man is a knave. This is a man of sense, or that is a fool." Thus far ought the father to judge, the rest belongs to the daughter. The tyrants, who exclaim that such maxims tend to disturb the good order of society, are those who, themselves, disturb it most. Let men rank according to their merit ; and let those hearts be united, that are objects of each other's choice. This is what the good order of society requires ; those who would confine it to birth or riches are the real disturbers of that order ; and ought to be rendered odious to the public, or punished, as enemies to society.

Justice requires that such abuses should be redressed ; it is the duty of every man to set himself in opposition to violence, and to strengthen the bonds of society.

If love be not predominant, prudence only directs the choice ; if passion prevail, nature has already determined it. So sacred is the law of nature, that no human being is permitted to transgress it, or can transgress it with impunity ; nor can any consideration of rank or fortune abrogate it, without involving mankind in guilt and misfortune.

I will content myself to recommend to you two things. Be virtuous and remember Julie.

I will not make use of any of those subtle arguments you have taught me to despise; and which, though they fill so many volumes, never yet made one man virtuous. Peace to those gloomy reasoners! To what ravishing delights their hearts are strangers! Leave, my friend, those idle moralists and consult your own breast. It is there you will always find a spark of sacred fire, which hath so often inflamed us with love for the sublimest virtue. It is there you will trace the lasting image of true beauty, the contemplation of which inspires us with a sacred enthusiasm; an image which the passions may continually defile, but never can efface. . . Would you know which is most truly desirable, riches or virtue? Think on that which interests us most in the perusal of history. Did you never covet the riches of Croesus, the honours of Caesar, the power of Nero, nor the pleasures of Heliogabalus? If they were happy, why did you not wish to be placed in the same situation? But they were not, you were sensible they were not happy; you were sensible they were vile and contemptible; and that bad men, however fortunate, are not objects of envy. What characters did you then contemplate with the greatest pleasure? What examples did you most admire? Which did you most desire to imitate? Inexpressible are the charms of ever-blooming virtue: it was the condemned Athenian drinking hemlock; it was Brutus, dying for his country; it was Regulus, in the midst of tortures; it was Cato, plunging his dagger in his breast. Those were the unfortunate heroes whose virtues excited your envy, while your own sensations bore witness of that real felicity they enjoyed, under their apparent misfortunes. Think not this sentiment peculiar to yourself ; it is the sentiment of all mankind, and that frequently in spite of themselves. That divine image of virtue, imprinted universally on the mind, displays irresistible charms even to the least virtuous. No sooner doth passion permit us to contemplate its beauty, but we wish to resemble it ; and if the most wicked of mankind could but change his being, he would choose to be virtuous.

But though it is not expected you should be put to the trials of a Cato, or a Regulus, yet every man ought to cherish a love for his country, resolution and integrity, and to keep his promise inviolable, even at the expense of his life. Private virtues are often the more sublime, as they less aspire to public approbation, but have their end in the testimony of a good conscience, which gives the virtuous a more solid satisfaction than the loudest applauses of the multitude. Hence you may see true greatness is confined to no one station of life, and that no man can be happy who is not the object of his own esteem.

I am convinced it is not good for man to be alone. Human minds must be united to exert their greatest strength, and the united force of friendly souls, like that of the collateral bars of an artificial magnet, is incomparably greater than the sum of their separate forces. This is thy triumph, celestial friendship ! But what is even friendship itself compared to that perfect union of souls, which connects the most perfect, the most harmonious amity, with ties an hundred times more sacred ? Where are the men whose ideas, gross as their appetites, represent the passion of love only as a fever in the blood, the effect of brutal instinct ?

I enter with a secret horror on this vast desert, the world ; whose confused prospect appears to me only as a frightful scene of solitude and silence. In vain my soul endeavours to shake off the universal restraint it lies under. It was the saying of a celebrated ancient that he was never less alone than when he was by himself : for my part, I am never alone but when I mix with the crowd, and am neither with you nor with anybody else. My heart would speak, but it feels there is none to hear : it is ready to answer, but no one speaks anything that regards it. I understand not the language of the country, and nobody here understands mine.

They talk about everything because everyone has something to say ; they examine nothing to the bottom, for fear of being tedious, but propose matters in a cursory manner, and treat them with rapidity : everyone gives his opinion and supports it in a few words ; no one attacks with virulence that of another, nor obstinately defends his own ; they discuss the point only for the sake of improvement, and stop before it comes to a dispute : everyone improves, everyone amuses himself, and they all part satisfied with each other ; even the philosopher himself carrying away something worthy his private meditation.

But, after all, what kind of knowledge do you think is to be gained from such agreable conversation ? To form a just judgement of life and manners ; to make a right use of society ; to know, at least, the people with whom we converse ; there is nothing, Julie, of all this : all they teach is to plead artfully the cause of falsehood, to confound by their philosophy, all the principles of virtue ; to throw a false colour, by the help of sophistry, on the passions and prejudices of mankind ; and to give a certain turn to error, agreable to the fashionable mode of thinking. It is not necessary to know the characters of men, but their interests, to guess their sentiments on any occasion. When a man talks on any subject, he rather expresses the opinions of his garb or his fraternity, than his own, and will change them as often as he changes his situation and circumstances. Thus men do not speak their own sentiments, but those they would instil into others, and the zeal which they affect is only the mask of interest.

You may imagine, however, that such persons as are unconnected and independent have, at least, a personal character and an opinion of their own. Not at all, they are only different machines, which never think for themselves, but are set a-going by springs.

As everyone considers his own particular interest, and none of them that of the public, and as the interests of individuals are always opposed, there is amongst them a perpetual clashing of parties and cabals, a continual ebb and flow of prepossessions and contrary opinions. Every club has its rules, its opinions, its principles, which are nowhere else admitted. An honest man at one house is a knave at the next door. The good, the bad, the beautiful, the ugly, truth, and even virtue itself have all only a limited and local existence. Such are the notions I have formed of great societies.

It was not the French in particular on whom I intended to animadvert. For if the characters of nations can be determined only by their difference, how can I, who have as yet no acquaintance with any other, pretend to draw the character of this ? I should not besides have been so indifferent as to fix on the metropolis for the place of observation. I am not ignorant that capital cities differ less from each other, than the national characters of the people, which are there in a great measure lost and confounded, as well from the influence of courts, all which bear a great resemblance to each other, as from the common consequence of living in a close and numerous society, which is everywhere nearly the same for all men, and prevails over the original and peculiar character of the country.

Were I to study the national characteristics of a people, I would repair to some of the more distant provinces, where the inhabitants still pursue their natural inclinations. I would proceed slowly and carefully through several of those provinces, and those at greatest distance from each other : from the difference I might observe between them, I would then trace the peculiar genius of each province; from what was theirs in common and not customary to other countries, I would trace the genius of the nation in general, and what appeared common to all nations, I should regard as characteristics of mankind in general.

The only way to come at the true manners of a nation is to study the private life of the most numerous order among them ; for to confine your observations to those who only personate assumed characters, is only to observe the actions of a company of comedians.

How comes it that in so opulent a city the poor people are so miserable? This question is well worth your asking : but it is not the people you converse with that are to resolve it. It is in the splendid apartments of the rich that the novice goes to learn the manners of the world ; but the man of sense and experience betakes himself to the cottages of the poor. These are the places for the detection of those iniquitous practices, that in polite circles are varnished over, and hid beneath a specious show of words. These are the places where one learns by what base and secret arts the rich and powerful snatch a crumb of black bread from the oppressed whom they feign to pity in public. You will learn many things in the garrets of a fifth floor, which are buried in profound silence in the suburbs of St. Germain ! You will find that many fine talkers would be struck dumb, if all those they have made unhappy were present to contradict their boasted pretensions to humanity.

I know the sight of misery that excites only fruitless pity is disagreeable ; and that even the rich turn away their eyes from the unhappy objects to whom they refuse relief : but money is not the only thing the unfortunate stand in need of ; and they are but indolent in well-doing who can exert themselves only with their purse in their hands. Consolation, advice, concern, friends, protection, these are all so many resources which compassion points out to those who are not rich, for the relief of the indigent. The oppressed often stand in need only of a tongue, to make known their complaints. They often want no more than a word they cannot speak, a reason they are ashamed to give, entrance at the door of a great man which they cannot obtain. The intrepid countenance of disinterested virtue may remove infinite obstacles, and the eloquence of a man of probity makes even a tyrant tremble in the midst of his guards.

If you would then act as a man, learn to descend again. Humanity, like a poor salutary stream, flows always downwards to its level; fertilising the humble vales, while it leaves dry those barren rocks, whose threatening heads cast a frightful shade, or tumbling headlong down involve the plain in ruins.

True love, as well as virtue, has this advantage, that it is rewarded by every sacrifice we make to it, and that we in some measure enjoy the privations we impose on ourselves, in the very idea of what they cost us, and of the motives by which we were induced.

Besides, if it is true, that love is the most delightful sensation that can enter into the human heart, everything that prolongs and fixes it, even at the expense of a thousand vexations, is still a blessing. If love is a desire, that is increased by obstacles, it ought never to be satisfied; it is better to preserve it at any rate, than that it should be extinguished in pleasure.

The idea of extinguished love is more terrifying to a tender heart, than that of an unhappy flame; and to feel a disgust for what we possess, is an hundred times worse than regretting what is lost.

I invoked that Being enthroned on high, whose pleasure supports or destroys, by means of our own strength, what free-will He has bestowed. "I eagerly," said I, "embrace the proffered good, of which thou art alone the author. I will be faithful because it is the chief duty which unites private families and society in general. I will be chaste, because it is the parent virtue which nourishes all the rest. I will adhere to everything relative to the order of nature which thou hast established, and to the dictates of reason which I derive from thee. I recommend my heart to thy protection, and my desires to thy guidance. Render all my actions conformable to my steadfast will, which is ever thine, and never more permit momentary error to triumph over the settled choice of my life."

Having finished this short prayer, I clearly perceived where I must hereafter resort for that power to resist my inclinations, which I could not derive from myself. I had never been devoid of religion, but perhaps I had better have been wholly so, than to have possessed one which was external and mechanical ; and which falsified the conscience without affecting the heart ; one which was confined to set forms ; and taught me to believe in God at stated hours, without thinking of him the remainder of my time.

Adore the Supreme Being, my worthy and prudent friend ; with one puff of breath you will be able to dissipate those chimeras of reason, which have a visionary appearance, and which fly like so many shadows, before immutable truth. Nothing exists but through Him, who is self-existent ; it is he who directs the tendency of justice, fixes the basis of virtue, and gives a recompense to a short life spent according to his will ; it is he who proclaims aloud to the guilty that their secret crimes are detected, and gives assurance to the righteous in obscurity, that their virtues are not without witness ; it is he, it is his inalterable substance that is the true model of those perfections, of which we all bear the image within us. It is in vain that our passions disfigure it ; its traces which are allied to the Infinite Being, ever present themselves to our reason, and serve to re-establish what error and imposture have perverted. These distinctions seem to me extremely natural ; common sense is sufficient to point them out. Everything which we cannot separate from the idea of divine essence, is God, all the rest is the work of men. It is by the contemplation of this divine model, that the soul becomes refined and exalted, that it learns to despise low desires, and to triumph over base inclinations. A heart impressed with these sublime truths is superior to the mean passions of human nature ; the idea of infinite grandeur subdues the pride of man ; the delight of contemplation abstracts him from gross desires ; and if the immense Being who is the subject of his thoughts had no existence, it would nevertheless be of use to exercise his mind in such meditations, in order to make him more master of himself, more vigorous, more discreet and more happy.

Do you require a particular instance of those vain subtleties framed by that self-sufficient reason, which only relies on its own strength ? Let us examine the arguments of those philosophers, those worthy advocates of a crime. Might one not conclude that, by a direct attack of the most holy and most solemn of all contracts, these dangerous disputants were determined at one stroke to annihilate human society in general, which is founded on the faith of engagements ? But let us consider how they exculpate secret adultery. It is because, say they, no mischief arises from it ; not even to the husband, who is ignorant of the wrong. But can they be certain that he will always remain ignorant of the injury offered him ? Is it sufficient to authorise perjury and infidelity, that they do no wrong to others? Is the mischief which the guilty do to themselves not sufficient to create an abhorrence of guilt? Is it no crime to be false to our word, to destroy as far as we are able, the obligation of oaths, and the most inviolable contracts? Is it no crime to form attachments, which occasion you to desire the misfortune, and to wish the death of another? Even the death of one whom we ought to love above others, and with whom we have sworn to live? Is not that state in itself an evil, which is productive of a thousand consequential crimes? Even good itself, if attended with so many mischiefs, would, for that reason only, be an evil.

It is not only the interest of husband and wife, but it is the common benefit of mankind, that the purity of marriage be preserved unsullied. The public are in some measure guarantees of a contract which passes in their presence; and we may venture to say that the honour of a modest woman is under the special protection of all good and worthy people. Whoever therefore dares to seduce her, sins; first because he has tempted her to sin, and that everyone is an accomplice in those crimes which he persuades others to commit: in the next place, he sins directly himself, because he violates the public and sacred faith of matrimony, without which no order or regularity can subsist in society.

The crime, say they, is secret, consequently no injury can result from it to anyone. If these philosophers believe the existence of a God and the immortality of the soul, can they call that crime secret, which has for its witness the Being principally offended and the only righteous judge? . . . If they do not however admit the omnipresence of the Divinity, yet how can they dare affirm that they do injury to no one? How can they prove that it is a matter of indifference to a parent to educate heirs who are strangers to his blood; to be encumbered perhaps with more children than he would otherwise have had, and to be obliged to distribute his fortune among those pledges of his dishonour, without feeling for them any sensations of parental tenderness, and natural affection? If we suppose these philosophers to be materialists, we have then a stronger foundation for opposing their tenets by the gentle dictates of nature, which plead in every breast against the principles of a vain philosophy. In short, if the body alone produces cogitation, and sentiment depends entirely on organs, will there not be a strict analogy between two beings of the same blood; will they not have a more violent attachment to each other?

Is it doing no injury therefore, in your opinion, to destroy or disturb this natural union by the mixing of adulterate blood, and to pervert the principle of that mutual affection, which ought to cement all the members of one family? Who would not shudder with horror at the thought of having one infant changed for another by a nurse? and is it a less crime to make such a change before the infant is born?

With regard to the pretended connections which may be formed in families by means of adultery and infidelity, it cannot be considered as a serious argument, but rather as an absurd and brutal mockery, which deserves no other answer than disdain and indignation. The treasons, the quarrels, the battles, the murders, with which this irregularity has in all ages pestered the earth, are sufficient proofs how far the peace and union of mankind is to be promoted by attachments founded in guilt. If any social principle results from this vile and despicable commerce, it may be compared to that which invites a band of robbers, and which ought to be destroyed and annulled, in order to ensure the safety of lawful communities.

Every man has a right by nature, to pursue what he thinks good, and avoid what he thinks evil, in all respects which are not injurious to others. When our life therefore becomes a misery to ourselves, and is of advantage to no one, we are at liberty to put an end to our being.

Let us hear what the philosophers say on this subject. First, they consider life as something which is not our own, because we hold it as a gift; but because it has been given to us, it is for that reason our own. Has not God given these sophists two arms? nevertheless when they are under fear of gangrene, they do not scruple to amputate one, or both if it is necessary.

They consider a man living upon earth, as a soldier placed on duty. God, say they, has fixed you in this world: why do you quit it without his leave? But you who argue thus, has he not stationed you in the town where you were born; why therefore do you quit it without his leave? Is not misery, of itself, a sufficient permission? Whatever station Providence has assigned me, whether it be in a regiment, or on the earth at large, he intended me to stay there while I found my station agreable, and to leave it when it became intolerable. This is the voice of nature and the voice of God. I agree that we must wait for an order; but when I die a natural death, God does not order me to quit life, he takes it from me: it is by rendering life insupportable, that he orders me to quit it. In the first case, I resist with all my force; in the second, I have the merit of obedience.

The grand error lies in making life of too much importance; as if our existence depended on it, and that death was a total annihilation. Our life is of no consequence in the sight of God; it is of no importance in the eyes of reason, neither ought it to be of any in our sight; and when we quit our body, we only lay aside an inconvenient habit.

The same sophists make it a question whether life can ever be an evil. But when we consider the multitude of errors, torments and vices with which it abounds, one would rather be inclined to doubt whether it can ever be a blessing. Guilt incessantly besieges the most virtuous of mankind. Every moment he lives, he is in danger of falling a prey to the wicked, or of being wicked himself. To struggle, and to endure, is his lot in this world; that of the dishonest man is to do evil, and to suffer. What is the chief occupation of a wise man in his life, but, if I may be allowed the expression, to collect himself inwardly and endeavour, even while he lives, to be dead to every object of sense? The only way by which wisdom directs us to avoid the miseries of human nature, is it not to detach ourselves from all earthly objects, from everything that is gross in our composition, to retire within ourselves, and to raise our thoughts to sublime contemplations? If therefore our misfortunes are derived from our passions and our errors, with what eagerness should we wish for a state which will deliver us both from the one and the other ?

But admitting it, in general, a benefit to mankind to crawl upon the earth with gloomy sadness ; I do not mean to intimate that the human race ought with one common consent to destroy themselves, and make the world one immense grave. While life is agreable to us, we earnestly wish to prolong it, and nothing but a sense of extreme misery can extinguish the desire of existence ; for we naturally conceive a violent dread of death, and this dread conceals the miseries of human nature from our sight. We drag a painful and melancholy life, for a long time before we can resolve to quit it ; but when once life becomes so unsupportable as to overcome the horror of death, then existence is evidently a great evil, and we cannot disengage ourselves from it too soon. Therefore, though we cannot exactly ascertain the point at which it ceases to be a blessing, yet at least we are certain that it is an evil long before it appears to be such, and with every sensible man the right of quitting life is by a great deal precedent to the temptation.

That is not all. After they have denied that life can be an evil, in order to bar our right of making away with ourselves, they confess immediately afterwards that it is an evil, by reproaching us with want of courage to support it. According to them it is cowardice to withdraw ourselves from pain and trouble, and they are none but dastards who destroy themselves. O Rome ! thou victrix of the world, what a race of cowards did thy empire produce ! Brutus, Cassius, and thou, great and divine Cato !

That paltry rhetoricians should ever attempt to prove that thou wert a coward, for having preferred death to a shameful existence!

Without doubt, it is an evidence of great fortitude to bear with firmness the misery which we cannot shun; none but a fool, however, will voluntarily endure evils which we cannot avoid without a crime, to suffer pain unnecessarily. He who has not resolution to deliver himself from a miserable being by a speedy death, is like one who would rather suffer a wound to mortify, than trust to the surgeon's knife for a cure.

Why should we be allowed to cure ourselves of the gout, and not to get rid of the misery of life? Do not both evils proceed from the same hand? Let them prove therefore that it is more justifiable to cure a transient disorder by the application of remedies, than to free ourselves from an incurable evil by putting an end to life. If we consider the object in view, it is in both cases to free ourselves from painful sensations; if we regard the means, both one and the other are equally natural; if we attend to the will of Providence, can we struggle against any evil, of which he is not the author? Can we deliver ourselves from any torment which his hand has not inflicted? What are the bounds which limit his power, and when is resistance lawful? Are we then to make no alteration in the condition of things, because everything is in the state he appointed? Must we do nothing in this life, for fear of infringing his laws, or is it in our power to break them if we would? No, the occupation of man is more great and noble. God did not give him life that he should remain supinely in a state of constant inactivity. But he gave him freedom to act, conscience to will, and reason to choose what is good. He has constituted him sole judge of all his actions. He has engraved the precept in his heart, "Do whatever you conceive to be for your own good, provided you thereby do injury to no one." If my sensations tell me that death is eligible, I resist his orders by an obstinate resolution to live, for by making death desirable, he directs me to put an end to my being.

According to you, you have a right to put an end to your being. Your proof is of a very singular nature; "Because I am disposed to die," say you, "I have a right to destroy myself." This is certainly a very convenient argument for villains of all kinds: they ought to be very thankful to you, for the arms with which you have furnished them; there can be no crimes, which, according to your arguments, may not be justified by the temptation to perpetrate them, and as soon as the impetuosity of passion shall prevail over the horror of guilt, their disposition to do evil will be considered as a right to commit it.

It is lawful therefore for you to quit life? What! were you placed here on earth to do nothing in this world? Did not heaven, when it gave you existence, give you some task or employment? If you have accomplished your day's work before evening, rest yourself for the remainder of the day, you have a right to do it; but let us see your work. What answer are you prepared to make the supreme judge, when he demands an account of your time? Thou unhappy wretch! point out to me that just man who can boast that he has lived long enough; let me learn from him in what manner I ought to have spent my days, to be at liberty to quit life.

You say : "Life is an evil." But search, examine into the order of things ; and see whether you can find any good which is not intermingled with evil. Does it therefore follow that there is no good in the universe, and can you confound what is in its own nature evil, with that which is only an evil accidentally ? You have confessed yourself, that the transitory and passive life of man is of no consequence and only bears respect to matter from which he will soon be disencumbered ; but his active and moral life, which ought to have most influence over his nature, consists in the exercise of free will. Life is an evil to a wicked man in prosperity, and a blessing to an honest man in distress ; for it is not its casual modification, but its relation to some final object, which makes it either good or bad.

You are weary of living ; and you say : "Life is an evil." Sooner or later you will receive consolation, and then you will say : "Life is a blessing." You will speak more truth, though not with better reason ; for nothing will have altered but yourself. Begin the alteration then from this day, and since all the evil you lament is in the disposition of your own mind, correct your irregular appetites and do not set your house on fire, to avoid the trouble of putting it in order.

"I endure misery, say you ; is it in my power to avoid suffering ?" You are wretched, you naturally endeavour to extricate yourself from misery. Let us see whether, for that purpose, it is necessary to die. . . Quiet, disquietude, regret and despair, are evils of short duration, which never take root in the mind, and experience always falsifies that bitter reflection, which makes us imagine our misery will have no end. I will go further ; I cannot imagine that the vices which contaminate us are more inherent in our nature, than the troubles we endure ; I not only believe that they perish with the body that gives them birth, but I think, beyond all doubt, that a longer life would be sufficient to reform mankind, and that many ages of youth would teach us that nothing is preferable to virtue.

However this may be, as the greatest part of our physical evils are incessantly increasing, the acute pains of the body, when they are incurable, may justify a man's destroying himself ; for all his faculties being distracted with pain, he ceases to be a man before he is dead, and does nothing more in taking away his life, than quit a body which encumbers him, and in which his soul is no longer resident.

But it is otherwise with the afflictions of the mind ; which let them be ever so acute, always carry their remedy with them. In fact, what is it that makes any evil tolerable ? nothing but its duration. What occasion is there therefore for any operation to remove troubles which die of course by their duration, the only circumstance which could render them supportable ? Have patience, and you will be cured.

Oh ! you will say, it doubles my afflictions, to reflect that they will cease at last ! This is the vain sophistry of grief ! an apophthegm void of reason, of propriety, and perhaps of sincerity. What an absurd motive of despair is the hope of terminating misery. And admitting any charm in grief, to make us in love with suffering, when we release ourselves from it by putting an end to our being, do we not at that instant incur all that we apprehend hereafter ?

Reflect thoroughly, young man; what are ten, twenty, thirty years, in competition with immortality? Pain and pleasure pass like a shadow! Life slides away in an instant; it is nothing of itself; its value depends on the use we make of it. The good that we have done is all that remains, and it is that alone which marks its importance.

You talk of the duties of a magistrate, and of a father of a family; and because you are not under those circumstances, you think yourself absolutely free. And you are then under no obligations to society, to whom you are indebted for your preservation, your talents, your understanding: do you owe nothing to your native country, and to those wretches who may need your assistance? Among the obligations you have enumerated, you have only omitted those of a man and a citizen.

You endeavour to justify yourself by examples. You presume to mention the Romans! Tell me, did Brutus die a lover in despair, and did Cato tear out his entrails for his mistress? Thou weak and abject man, what resemblance is there between Cato and thee?

How meanly you judge of the Romans, if you imagine that they thought themselves at liberty to quit life so soon as it became a burden to them. When Rome was no more, it was lawful for the Romans to give up their lives; they had discharged their duties on earth, they had no longer any country to defend, they were therefore at liberty to dispose of their lives, and to obtain that freedom for themselves, which they could not recover for their country. Their death was an additional tribute to the glory of the Roman name, since none of them beheld a sight above all others most dishonourable, that of a true citizen stooping to an usurper.

But thou, what art thou ? What hast thou done ? Know that a death such as you meditate, is shameful and surreptitious. It is a theft committed on mankind in general. Before you quit life, return the benefits you have received from every individual. But, say you, I have no attachments, I am useless in the world. O thou young philosopher ! art thou ignorant that thou canst not move a single step without finding some duty to fulfil ; and that every man is useful to society, even by means of his existence alone ?

What a pleasing and affecting scene is a simple and well-regulated family, where order, peace, and innocence reign throughout ; where, without pomp or retinue, everything is assembled, which can contribute to the real felicity of mankind !

It is no longer a house for shew, but for convenience. Everything here is pleasant and agreable ; everything breathes an air of plenty and propriety, without an appearance of pomp and luxury. They have throughout substituted the useful in the place of the agreable, and yet the agreable has gained by the alteration.

Having a great deal of land, which they cultivate with the utmost industry, they require, besides the servants in the yard, a great number of day labourers, which procures them the pleasure of maintaining a great number of people without any inconvenience to themselves.

Mme. de Wolmar does not think it sufficient to reward their industry by giving them money, but she thinks herself bound to do further services to those who have contributed to hers. Labourers, domestics, all who serve her, if it be but for a day, become her children.

Here, the choice of domestics is considered as an article of importance. They do not regard them merely as mercenaries, from whom they only require a stipulated service, but as members of a family, which, should they be ill-chosen, might be ruined by that means. The first thing they require of them is to be honest, the next is to love their master, and the third to serve him to his liking. They employ some days in teaching them their duty with a great deal of care and patience. The service is so simple, so equal and so uniform, the master and mistress are so little subject to whims and caprice, and the servants so soon conceive an affection for them, that their business is soon learned. Their condition is agreable, but they are not suffered to be enervated by idleness, the parent of all vice.

When a domestic first enters into their service, he receives the common wages; but those wages are augmented every year by a twentieth part: so that at the end of twenty years, they will be more than doubled. This is a certain expedient of making servants grow continually more and more careful, and of attaching them to you, by attaching yourself to them. There is not only prudence but justice in such a provision.

Though there is but one table among all the servants, yet there is but little communication between the men and the women, and this they consider as a point of great importance. Too close a connection between the two sexes frequently occasions mischief.

They do not, to prevent any dangerous intimacy between the two sexes, restrain them by positive rules which they might be tempted to violate in secret, but without seeming intention, they establish good customs, which are more powerful than authority itself. They do not forbid any intercourse between them, but it is contrived in such a manner that they have no occasion or inclination to see each other. This is effectuated by making their business, their habits, their tastes, and their pleasures entirely different. Julie insists that neither love nor conjugal union is the result of a continual commerce between the sexes. In her opinion, husband and wife were designed to live together, but not to live in the same manner. They ought to act in concert, but not to do the same things. "The kind of life," says she, "which would delight the one, would be insupportable to the other ; the inclinations which nature has given them, are as different as the occupations she has assigned them : they differ in their amusements as much as in their duties. In a word, each contributes to the common good by different ways, and the proper distribution of their several cares and employments, is the strongest tie that cements their union."

Every Sunday, after evening service, the women meet again. They chat, sing, run or play at some little game of skill. Refreshment is brought. Wine is almost always excluded, and the men, who are rarely admitted at this little female party, never are present at this collation.

To keep the women in order would signify nothing, if the men were not likewise under proper regulations. In the commonwealth, citizens are kept in order by principles of morality and virtue ; but how are we to keep servants and mercenaries under proper regulations, otherwise than by force and constraint ? The art of a master consists in disguising this restraint under the veil of pleasure and interest. The habit of frequenting public houses, the company of loose women, soon render them unserviceable to their masters, and unprofitable to themselves, and by teaching them a thousand vices, make them unfit for servitude, and unworthy of liberty.

To remedy this inconvenience, they endeavour to keep them at home by the same motives that induce them to go abroad. Why do they go abroad ? To drink and play at a public house. They drink and play at home. All the difference is that the wine costs them nothing, that they do not get drunk, and that there are some winners at play, without any losers.

Behind the house is a shady walk, where they have fixed the lists. There in summer time, the men meet every Sunday after sermon time, to play in little detached parties, not for money, for it is not allowed, nor for wine, which is given them, but for a prize furnished by their master's generosity. They are not confined to one particular game, but they change them, that one man, who happens to excel in a particular game, may not carry off all the prizes, and that they may grow stronger and more dexterous by a variety of exercises. At one time, the contest is who shall first reach a mark at the other end of the walk ; at another time it is who shall throw the same stone farthest; then again it is who shall carry the same weight longest. This custom has imperceptibly become a kind of show in which the actors, being animated by the presence of the spectators, prefer the glory of applause to the lucre of the prize. As these exercises make them more active and vigorous, they set a greater value on themselves, and being accustomed to estimate their importance from their own intrinsic worth, they prize honour beyond money.

In the winter, their pleasures vary as well as their labours. On a Sunday, all the servants in the family and even the neighbours, men and women indiscriminately, meet after service time in a hall where there is a good fire, some wine, fruits, cakes and a fiddle to which they dance.

It has been said that no man is a hero in the eyes of his *valet de chambre*; perhaps not; but every worthy man will enjoy his servants' esteem: which sufficiently proves that heroism is only a vain phantom and that nothing is solid but virtue.

There is not only a proper subordination among those of inferior station, but a perfect harmony among those of equal rank; and this is not the least difficult part of domestic economy.

Who does not see, that in this family, they have not even an idea of any such difficulty, so much does the union among the several members proceed from their attachment to the head. Is it not very natural, that the children of the same father should live together like brethren? This is what they tell us every day at church, without making us feel the sentiment; and this is what the domestics in this family feel, without being told it.

This disposition to good fellowship is owing to a choice of proper subjects. After having made the best assortment in their power, they unite them as it were by the services which they oblige each to render the other, and they contrive that it shall be the real interest of everyone to be beloved by his fellow servants.

Riches do not make a man rich, as is well observed in some romance. The wealth of a man is not in his coffers, but in the use he makes of what he draws out of them ; for our possessions do not become our own, but by the uses to which we allot them, and abuses are always more inexhaustible than riches ; whence it happens that our enjoyments are not in proportion to our expenses but depend on the best regulation of them. An idiot may toss ingots of gold into the sea, and say he has enjoyed them : but what comparison is there between such an extravagant enjoyment, and that which a wise man would have derived from the least part of their value ? Order and regularity, which multiply and perpetuate the use of riches, are alone capable of converting the enjoyment of them into felicity.

Are the most wealthy the most happy ? No : how then does wealth contribute to felicity ? But every well-regulated family is emblematic of the master's mind. Gilded ceilings, luxury and magnificence, only serve to shew the vanity of those who display such parade ; whereas whenever you see order without melancholy, peace without slavery, plenty without profusion, you may say with confidence, the master of this house is a happy being.

For my own part, I think the most certain sign of true content is a domestic and retired life, and that they who are continually resorting to others in quest of happiness, do not enjoy it at home.

There are many simple and sublime duties, which few people can relish and fulfil. Such are those of the master of a family, for which the air and bustle of the world give him a disgust, and which he never discharges properly when he is only inflamed by motives of avarice and interest. Some think themselves excellent masters, and are only careful economists; their income may thrive, and their family nevertheless be in a bad condition. They ought to have more enlarged views to direct an administration of such importance, so as to give it a happy issue. The first thing to be attended to in the due regulation of a family, is to admit none but honest people, who will not have any secret intention to disturb that regularity. But are honesty and servitude so compatible, that we may hope to find servants who are honest men? No, if we would have them, we must not enquire for them, but we must make them; and none who are not men of integrity themselves are capable of making others honest.

The grand art by which the masters make their servants what they would desire them to be, is to appear themselves before them what they really are. Their behaviour is always frank and open. As their servants never see them do anything but what is just, reasonable and equitable, they do not consider justice as a tax on the poor, as a yoke on the unhappy, and as one of the evils of their condition. The care they take never to let the labourers come in vain, and lose their day's work in seeking after their wages, teaches their servants to set a just value on time.

You never perceive any sullenness or mutiny in the

discharge of their duty, because there is never any haughtiness or capriciousness in the orders they receive ; nothing is required of them but what is reasonable and expedient, and their master and mistress have too much respect for the dignity of human nature, even in a state of servitude, to put them upon any employment which may debase them. Moreover, nothing here is reckoned mean but vice, and whatever is reasonable and necessary is deemed honourable and becoming.

It requires a sound mind to be able to enjoy the pleasures of retirement ; the virtuous, only, being capable of amusing themselves with their family concerns ; and of voluntarily secluding themselves from the world : if there be on earth any such thing as happiness, they undoubtedly enjoy it in such a state. But the means of happiness are nothing to those who know not how to make use of them ; and we never know in what true happiness consists, till we have acquired a taste for its enjoyment.

If I were desired to speak with precision as to the reason why the inhabitants of this place are happy, I should think I could not answer with greater propriety than to say, it is because *they here know how to live* ; not in the sense in which these words would be taken in France, where it would be understood that they had adopted certain customs and manners in vogue : no, but they have adopted such manners as are most agreable to human life ; to that life which extends beyond itself, and is not given up for lost even in the hour of death.

Julie has a father who is anxious for the honour and interests of his family : she has children for whose subsistence it is necessary to provide. This ought to be the chief care of man in a state of society; and was therefore the first in which Julie and her husband were united. When they began housekeeping they examined into the state of their fortunes; not considering so much whether they were proportioned to their rank, as to their wants; and seeing that they were sufficient for the provision of an honourable family, they had not so bad an opinion of their children, as to be fearful lest the patrimony they had to leave would not content them. They applied themselves therefore rather to improve their present, than acquire a larger fortune.

It is true that an estate which is not augmented is liable to many accidents by which it will naturally diminish: but if this were a sufficient motive to begin increasing, when would it cease to be a pretext for a constant augmentation? Must it be divided among several children? Be it so, must they be all idle? Will not the industry of each be a supplement to his share, and ought it not to be considered in the partition? It is thus that insatiable avarice makes its way under the mask of prudence and leads to vice under the cloak of its own security.

The master of this house possesses but a moderate fortune, according to the estimation of the world; but in reality I hardly know anybody more opulent. There is indeed no such thing as absolute wealth: that term signifying only the relation between the wants and possessions of those who are rich. One man is rich, though possessing only an acre of land; another is a beggar in the midst of heaps of gold. Luxury and caprice have no bounds, and make more persons poor than real wants.

I was at first struck with a peculiarity in the economy of this house, where there appeared so much ease, freedom and gaiety, in the midst of order and diligence; the great fault of well-regulated houses being that they always wear an air of gloominess and restraint. The extreme solicitude also of the heads of the family looks too much like avarice. Everything about them seems constrained. Such slavish fathers of families cannot be said to live for themselves, but for their children; without considering that they are not only fathers but men, and that they ought to set their children an example how to live prudent and happy. More judicious maxims are adopted here. M. de Wolmar thinks one of the principal duties of a father of a family is to make his house, in the first place, agreable, that his children may delight in their home, and that seeing their father happy, they may be tempted to tread in his footsteps. Another of his maxims, and which he often repeats, is that the gloomy and sordid lives of fathers and mothers are almost always the first cause of the ill-conduct of children.

As to Julie, she obeys, without scruple, the dictates of her heart. Can a mind so susceptible as hers be insensible of pleasure? On the contrary, she delights in every amusement, nor refuses to join in any diversion that promises to be agreable; but her pleasures are the pleasures of Julie. She neglects neither her own convenience nor the satisfaction of those who are dear to her. She esteems nothing superfluous that may contribute to the happiness of a sensible mind: but censures everything as such, that serves only to make a figure in the eyes of others.

As the first step to virtue is to forbear doing ill, so the first step to happiness is to be free from pain. These two maxims, which well understood, would render precepts of morality in a degree useless, are favourable ones with Mme. de Wolmar. She is extremely affected by the misfortunes of others; and it would be as difficult for her to be happy with wretched objects about her, as it would be for an innocent man to preserve his virtue and live in the midst of vice. She has none of that barbarous piety, which is satisfied with turning away its eye from the miserable objects it might relieve. On the contrary, she makes it her business to seek out such objects: it is the existence, and not the presence, of the unhappy which gives her affliction. It is not sufficient for her to be ignorant that there are any such; it is necessary to her quiet that she should be assured there are none miserable; at least within her sphere of charity: for it would be unreasonable to extend her concern beyond her own neighbourhood, and to make her happiness depend on the welfare of all mankind. She takes care to inform herself of the necessities of all that live near her, and interests herself in their relief as if their wants were her own. She knows everyone personally, includes them all, as it were, in her family, and spares no pains to banish, or alleviate, those misfortunes and afflictions to which human life is subject.

What pleases me most in the solicitude which prevails here regarding the happiness of others is, that their benevolence is always exerted with prudence, and is never abused. We do not always succeed in our benevolent intentions; but on the contrary, some people imagine they are doing great services, who are, in reality, doing great injuries, and with a view to a little manifest good, are guilty of much unforeseen evil. Mme. de Wolmar indeed possesses, in an eminent degree, a qualification very rare, even among women of the best character ; I mean an exquisite discernment in the distribution of her favours. Whoever hath committed an infamous or wicked action, hath nothing to hope for from her but justice, and her pardon, if he has offended her ; but never that favour and protection, which she can bestow on a worthier object.

Her protection is never refused to anyone, who really stands in need of, and deserves to obtain it : but for those who desire to raise themselves through fickleness or ambition only, she can very seldom be prevailed upon to give herself any trouble. The natural business of man is to cultivate the earth, and subsist on its produce. The peaceful inhabitant of the country needs only know in what happiness consists, to be happy. His situation is the only necessary, the only useful one in life. He is never unhappy, but when others tyrannise over him, or seduce him by their vices. In agriculture and husbandry consists the real prosperity of a country, the greatness and strength which a people desire from themselves, that which depends not on other nations, which is not obliged to attack others for its own preservation, but is productive of the surest means of its own defense. In making an estimate of the strength of a nation, a superficial observer would visit the court, the prince, his ports, his troops, his magazines, and his fortified towns ; but the true politician would take a survey of the country, and visit the cottages of the husbandmen. The former would only see what is already executed, but the latter what was capable of being put into execution.

On this principle they contribute as much as possible to make the peasants happy in their condition, without ever assisting them to change it. Care is exerted in teaching them to honour their native condition, by seeming to honour it themselves.

Mme. de Wolmar's great maxim is, therefore, never to encourage anyone to change his condition, but to contribute all in her power to make everyone happy in his present station ; being particularly solicitous to prevent the happiest of all situations, that of a peasant in a free state, from being despised in favour of other employments.

I, one day, made an objection on this subject, founded on the different talents which nature seems to have bestowed on mankind, in order to fit them for different occupations, without any regard to their birth. This she obviated, however, by observing that there were two more material things to be consulted, before talents : these were virtue and happiness. "Man," said she, "is too noble a being to be made a mere tool of for the use of others : he ought not to be employed in what he is fit for, without consulting how far such employment is fit for him ; for we are not made for our stations, but our stations for us. In the right distribution of things therefore, we should not adapt men to circumstances, but circumstances to men ; we should not seek that employment for which a man is best adapted, but that which is best adapted to make him virtuous and happy. For it can never be right to destroy one human soul for the temporal advantage of others, nor to make any man a villain for the use of honest people.

"In order to pursue our talents, we must know what they are and it is no easy matter to discover the talents with which nature hath severally endowed us. There is nothing so equivocal as the genius frequently attributed to youth. Real talent, or true genius, is attended with a certain simplicity of disposition, which makes it less restless and enterprising, less ready to thrust itself forward than a superficial and false one; which is nevertheless generally mistaken for the true, and consists only in a vain desire of making a figure without talents to support it. One of these geniuses hears the drum beat, and is immediately in idea a general; another sees a palace, and imagines himself an architect. But it is not enough to be sensible of the bent of our genius, unless we are willing to pursue it. Will a prince turn coachman, because he is expert at driving a set of horses? Will a duke turn cook, because he is ingenious at inventing ragouts? Our talents all tend to preferment; no one pretends to those which would fit him for an inferior station: do you think this is agreable to the order of nature? Suppose everyone sensible of his own talents and as willing to employ them, how is it possible? How could they surmount so many obstacles? . . . He who finds in himself the want of abilities, would call in subtlety and intrigue to his aid, which another, more sure of himself, would disdain. In multiplying indiscreetly the number of professors and academicians, true merit is lost in the crowd, and the honours, due to the most ingenious, are always bestowed on the most intriguing. Did there exist a society wherein the rank and employment of its respective members were exactly calculated to their talents and personal merit, everyone might there aspire to the place he should be most fit for ; but it is necessary to conduct ourselves by other rules, and give up that of abilities, in societies where the vilest of all talents is the only one that leads to fortune.

"I will add further : I cannot be persuaded of the utility of having so many different talents displayed. It seems necessary, the number of persons so qualified should be exactly proportionate to the wants of society. I am apt to think therefore, that great talents in men are like great virtues in drugs, which nature has provided to cure our maladies, though its intention certainly was that we should never stand in need of them. In the vegetable kingdom there are plants which are poisonous ; in the brutal, animals that would tear us to pieces ; and among mankind there are those who possess talents no less destructive to their species. Besides, if everything were to be put to that use for which its qualities seem best adapted, it might be productive of more harm than good in the world. There are thousands of simple, honest people, who have no occasion for a diversity of great talents ; supporting themselves better by their simplicity than others with all their ingenuity. But, in proportion as their morals are corrupted, their talents are displayed, as if to serve as a supplement to the virtues they have lost, and to oblige the vicious to be useful in spite of themselves."

Another subject on which we differed, was the relieving of beggars. I represented to her that this practice tended to multiply beggars and vagabonds, who take pleasure in that idle life, and by rendering themselves a burthen on society, deprive it of their labour.

"I see very well," says she, "you have imbibed prejudices by living in great cities, and some of those maxims by which you complaisant reasoners love to flatter the hard-heartedness of the wealthy. My husband has always appeared to despise these arguments. 'We permit,' says he, 'and even support at a great expense, a multitude of useless professions; many of which serve only to spoil and corrupt our manners. Now, to look upon the profession of a beggar as a trade, it serves to excite in us those sentiments of humanity which ought to unite all mankind. A great number of beggars may be burthensome to a state: but of how many professions, which are tolerated and encouraged, may we not say the same? It belongs to the legislature and administration to take care there should be no beggars; but, in order to make them lay down their trade, is it necessary to make all other ranks of people inhuman and unnatural?' "For my part," continued Julie, "without knowing what the poor may be to the state, I know they are all my brethren, and that I cannot, without thinking myself inexcusable, refuse them the small relief they ask of me. I know too much of life, to be ignorant how many misfortunes may reduce an honest man to such a situation; and how can I be sure, that an unhappy stranger, who comes, in the name of God, to implore my assistance, and to beg a poor morsel of bread, is not such an honest man, ready to perish for want, and whom my refusal may drive to despair? A halfpenny and a piece of bread are refused to nobody; should they meet with the same relief at every house which can afford it, it would be sufficient to support them on their journey. But supposing this was not enough to yield them any real help, it is at least a proof that we take some part in their distress; a sort of salutation that softens the rigour of refusing them more. A halfpenny and a morsel of bread cost little more and are a more civil answer than a mere *God help you*; which is too often the only thing bestowed, as if the gifts of Providence were not in the hands of men, or that heaven had any other store on earth than what is laid up in the coffers of the rich. In short, whatever we ought to think of such unfortunate wretches, and though nothing should in justice be given to common beggars, we ought at least, out of respect to ourselves, to take some notice of suffering humanity, and not harden our hearts at the sight of the miserable."

Julie's mind and body are equally sensible. The same delicacy prevails as well in her senses as her sentiments. She was formed to know and taste every pleasure; but then her method of enjoyment resembles the austerity of self-denial: not indeed of that afflicting and painful self-denial, which is hurtful to nature, and which its author rejects as ridiculous homage; but of that slight and moderate restraint, by which the empire of reason is preserved; and which serves as a whet to pleasure by preventing disgust. Thus her mind preserves its first vigour: her taste is not spoiled by use; she has no need to excite it by excess.

A still nobler object, which she proposes to herself from the exercise of this virtue, is that of remaining always mistress of herself, and to subject her inclinations to rule. This is a new way to be happy; for it is certain that we enjoy nothing with so little inquietude, as what we can part from without pain; and if the philosopher be happy, it is because he is the man from whom fortune can take the least.

"Life is indeed short," says she, "which is a reason for enjoying it to the end, and managing its duration in such a manner as to make the most of it. If one day's indulgence and satiety deprives us of a whole year's taste for enjoyment, it is bad philosophy to pursue our desires so far as they may be ready to lead us."

"Besides the constitution common to its species, every child at birth possesses a peculiar temperament, which determines its genius and character; and which it is improper either to prevent or restrain; the business of education being only to model and bring to perfection. Nature makes no mistakes. All the vices imputed to malignity of disposition are only the effect of the bad form it hath received. There is not a villain upon earth, whose natural propensity, well directed, might not have been productive of great virtues; nor is there a wrong-head in being, that might not have been of use to himself in society, had his natural talents taken a certain bias, just as deformed and monstrous images are rendered beautiful and proportionable, by placing them in a proper point of view. Everything tends to the common good in the universal system of nature. Every man has the place assigned in the best order and arrangement of things; the business is to find out that place, and not to disturb such order. What must be the consequence then of an education begun in the cradle, and carried on always in the same manner, without regard to the vast diversity of temperaments and geniuses in mankind? Useless or hurtful instructions would be given to the greater part, while at the same time they are deprived of such as would be most useful and convenient; nature would be confined on every side, and the greatest qualities of the mind defaced, in order to substitute in their place mean and little ones, of no utility. By using indiscriminately the same means with different talents, the one serves to deface the other and all are confounded together. In a word, in return for so much pains indiscreetly taken, all these little prodigies become wits without sense, and men, without merit, remarkable only for their weakness and insignificancy."

Learn not always to depend on your own sagacity on difficult occasions; but on that Being whose omnipotence is equal to his wisdom, and who knows how to direct us in everything aright. The greatest defect in human wisdom, even in that which has only virtue for its object, is a too great confidence, which makes us judge by the present of the future, and of our whole lives from the experience of a single moment. We perceive ourselves resolute one instant, and therefore conclude we shall always be so. The modest language of true fortitude is: "*I had resolution on this or that occasion*;" but he who boasts of his present security knows not how weak he may prove on the next trial.

How vain are all our projects, how absurd our reasonings in the eyes of that Being, who is not confined to time or space! Man is so weak as to disregard things which are placed at a distance from him: he sees only the objects which immediately surround him; change his notions of things as the point of sight is changed from whence he views them. We judge of the future from what agrees with us now, without knowing how far that which pleases today may be disagreable tomorrow; we depend on ourselves, as if we were always the same, and yet are changing every day. Who can tell if they shall always desire what they now wish for? If they shall be tomorrow what they are today, if external objects and even a change in the constitution of the body may not vary the modification of their minds, and if we may not be made miserable by the very means we have concerted for our happiness?

I have heard a good deal of argument against the free-agency of man, and despise all its sophistry. A casuist may take what pains he will to prove that I am no free agent, my innate sense of freedom constantly destroys his arguments: for whatever choice I make after deliberation, I feel plainly that it depended only on myself to have made the contrary. Indeed, all the scholastic subtilties I have heard on this head are futile and frivolous; because they prove too much, are equally used to oppose truth and falsehood, and whether a man be a free agent or not, serve equally to prove one or the other. With this kind of reasoners, the Deity himself is not a free agent, and the word liberty is in fact a term of no meaning. They triumph, not in having solved the difficulty, but in having substituted a chimera in its room.

I don't believe that after having provided in every

shape for the wants of man in his formation, God interests himself in an extraordinary manner for one person more than another. Those who abuse the common aids of Providence are unworthy such assistance, and those who made good use of them have no occasion for any other. Such a partiality appears to me injurious to divine justice. You will say this severe and discouraging doctrine may be deduced from the holy scripture. Be it so. Is it not my first duty to honour my Creator? In whatever veneration then I hold the sacred text, I hold its author in a still greater; and I could sooner be induced to believe the Bible corrupted or unintelligible, than that God can be malevolent or unjust.

But does it follow from thence that prayer is useless? God forbid that I should deprive myself of that resource. Every act of the understanding which raises us to God carries us above ourselves; in imploring his assistance we learn to experience it. It is not his immediate act that operates on us, it is we that improve ourselves by raising our thoughts in prayer to him. All that we ask aright, he bestows; and we acquire strength in confessing our weakness. But if we abuse this ordinance and turn mystics instead of raising ourselves to God, we are lost in our own wild imaginations; in seeking grace, we renounce reason; in order to obtain of heaven one blessing, we trample under foot another, and in obstinately persisting that heaven should enlighten our hearts, we extinguish the light of our understandings. But who are we that we should insist on the Deity's performing miracles, when we please, in our favour?

I have heard you often censure the ecstasies of the

pietists : but do you know from whence they arise ? From allotting a longer time to prayer than is consistent with the weakness of human nature. Hence the spirits are exhausted, the imagination takes fire, they see visions, they become inspired and prophetical ; nor is it then in the power of the understanding to stop the progress of fanaticism.

I have condemned indeed the ecstasies of the mystics, and condemn them still, when they serve to detach us from our duty ; and by raising in us a disgust against an active life by the charm of contemplation, seduce us into that state of quietism which you imagine me so near, and from which I believe myself nevertheless to be as far distant as yourself.

I know very well that to serve God is not to pass our lives on our knees in prayer ; that it is to discharge on earth those obligations which our duty requires.

We ought first to perform the duties of our station, and then pray when we have time.

I have lived and I die in the Protestant communion, whose maxims we deduced from scripture and reason ; concerning which my heart hath always confirmed what my lips uttered. I have always sincerely sought what was most conformable to truth, and the glory of my Creator. I may have been deceived in my research ; I have not the vanity to think I have always been in the right. I may indeed have been constantly in the wrong ; but my intention has been invariably good. If God did not vouchsafe to enlighten my understanding farther, he is too merciful and just to demand of me an account of what he has not committed to my care.

God is more merciful than I am criminal, and my

confidence increases as I find I approach nearer to him.

To what punishment can a just God condemn me? The reprobates, it is said, hate him. Must he not first make me not to love him? No, I fear not to be found one of that number. O thou great eternal Being! Supreme intelligence! Source of life and happiness! Creator! Preserver! Father! Lord of Nature! God powerful and good, of whose existence I never doubted a moment, and under whose eye I have always delighted to live! I know, I rejoice, that I am going to appear before thy throne. In a few days, my soul, delivered from its earthly tabernacle, shall begin to pay thee more worthily that immortal homage which will constitute my happiness to all eternity. I look upon what I shall be, till that moment comes, as nothing. Those who sleep on the bosom of a father, are in no fear of being awakened.

THE CONFESSIONS

While he was still at Montmorency, after the success of The New Héloïse, *and while he was finishing* Emile, *from which he expected to make a little money, Rousseau, dreaming of retirement, reserved for himself* "an occupation which would fill his empty solitude," *with no intention of publication during his lifetime. This was to be* "the memoirs of my life." *He wished to make of them* "a work unique for its truthfulness, so that the world might possess for the first time the portrait of a man 'painted after nature' . . ." *The events which made necessary his flight interrupted this plan and deprived him of a great part of his documents, upon which he counted for refreshing his wavering memory, too often led astray by his perpetual reveries. Nevertheless, he started this work in* 1765 *in the solitude of Motiers-Travers in Switzerland. He then gave to his Memoirs the name of* Confessions. *Again interrupted by his flight from Switzerland to London, then by the mental panic which followed, he returned to the* Confessions, *in April* 1769, *and finished them in December* 1770, *in Paris. But the story does not go farther than the end of October* 1770, *the time of his departure from Switzerland. He gave up writing of what followed, in order not to have to relive the sufferings of those years. By an admirable mastery over his mind, he was able to keep the last parts of his work free from any suggestion of the deliriums of anguish which possessed him; we only catch a glimpse of them in the last page; and it is perhaps because they were perceptible then that he decided not to continue. A still higher strength of character kept him from taking revenge on his enemies, whom he could easily have pilloried, and who expected this as was shown by the slanderous fury of certain among them. The* Confessions *were published after Rousseau's death, the first six books in* 1782; *the other six in* 1789.

No other of Rousseau's works had so much influence on the French literature of the following century. His book was the mother of the Confessions *of the first romanticists, of the* René *of Chateaubriand and the* Adolphe *of Benjamin Constant. It opened into the art of the novel the recesses of the inner life.*

I felt before I thought ; 'tis the common fate of humanity.

Figure to yourself a timid and docile character in common life, but ardent, haughty, invincible in his passions ; a child always governed by the voice of reason, always treated with mildness, equity, and complaisance ; who had not even the idea of injustice, and who, for the first time, experiences a terrible one, from those, precisely, he most cherishes and respects. What a perverting of ideas ! what a disorder in the sentiments ! what confusion in the heart, in the brain, in all one's little being, intelligent and moral ! I say, let anyone imagine to himself all this, if possible ; for as to myself, I am not capable of discovering or following the least trace of what passed in me at the time.

I had not sense enough to feel how much appearances condemned me, and to put myself in the place of others ; I kept to my own, and all I felt was the rigour of a dreadful chastisement for a crime I had not committed. The soreness of my body, though severe, I scarcely felt ; I only felt indignation, rage, and despair. My cousin, in almost a like case, who had been punished for an involuntary fault as a premeditated act, grew furious by my example, and raised himself in a manner to unite with me. Both in the same bed embraced each other with convulsive transports ; we were suffocated ; and when our young hearts, a little eased, could breathe out their indignation, we sat up in our bed, and began both of us crying out an hundred times, with all our force : *Carnifex ! Carnifex ! Carnifex !*

I feel in writing this my pulse still rise ; these moments would be continually present, were I to live an hundred thousand years. This first sentiment of violence and of injustice is so deeply graven on my soul, that every resembling idea brings back my first emotion ; and this sentiment, relative to me in its origin, has taken such a consistence, and is so far from personal interest, that my heart is inflamed at the sight or recital of an unjust action, whatever may be its object or wheresoever it may be committed, as if the effect fell on me. When I read the history of a cruel tyrant, the subtle black actions of a knavish priest, I could set off heartily to stab these miscreants, though I should perish an hundred times in the attempt. I have often sweated in pursuing and stoning a cock, a cow, a dog, an animal, I saw torment another, only because he knew himself to be the strongest. This emotion may be natural to me, and I believe it is ; but the profound remembrance of the first injustice I suffered, was too long and too strongly annexed not to have greatly strengthened it.

Reflections on myself have not a little contributed to keep my heart sound. I drew from them this great maxim of morality, the only one perhaps in practical use, to shun those situations which put our duty in opposition with our interests, and which shew us our good in the misfortunes of others ; and that in such situations, however sincere a love for virtue we bear, we weaken sooner or later without perceiving it, and become unjust and wicked in fact, without ceasing to be just and innocent at the heart.

This maxim, strongly imprinted on my heart, and put in practice in all my conduct, though a little late, is one of those which have given me the most whimsical and foolish appearance, not only among the public, but more particularly among my acquaintance. I have been charged with being original, and not doing like others. In fact, I thought little of doing either like others or otherwise than they did. I sincerely desired to do what was right. I avoided, as much as possible, those situations which procured me an interest contrary to that of another man, and consequently, a secret, though involuntary desire of hurting that man.

The sophism which more than once ruined me is that of the greatest part of mankind, who complain of want of power, when it is too late to make use of it. Virtue is dearly bought by our own fault; if we were always prudent, we should seldom have occasion of virtue. But inclinations which might be easily surmounted, drag us without resistance; we yield to light temptations whose danger we despise. Insensibly we fall into perilous situations from which we might easily have preserved ourselves, but from which we cannot extricate ourselves without heroic efforts which affright us; so we fall at last into the abyss, in saying to God, "Why hast Thou made me so weak?" But, in spite of us, He replies to our consciences, "I made you too weak to get out of the gulf, because I made you strong enough not to fall into it."

In the successive order of my inclinations I had always been too high or too low; Achilles or Thersites; sometimes a hero, sometimes a villain. M. Gaime took the pains to put me in my proper place, and to shew me to myself without sparing or discouraging me. He spoke to me very honourably of my talents and my genius ; but he added that he saw obstacles arise from them which would prevent me from making the best of them, so that they would, according to him, serve me much less in the attainment of fortune, than in resources to do without it. He painted me the true picture of human life, of which I had but wrong ideas : he explained to me, how in adversity a wise man may always attain happiness, and gain that wind which blows him there ; how there is no happiness without prudence, and how it is that prudence belongs to every condition. He greatly deadened my admiration for grandeur, in proving to me that those who lorded it over others were neither wiser nor happier than they were. He told me one thing which often occurs to my memory ; and that is, if each man could read the hearts of others, there would be more people would wish to descend than ascend. This reflection, whose reality strikes, and has nothing forced, has been very useful to me in the course of my life, in making me keep to my lot peaceably. He gave me the first true ideas of honesty, which my bombastic genius had only known to excess. He made me understand, that the enthusiasm for sublime virtue was of little use in society ; that in aiming too high you are subject to fall ; that the continuity of little duties well fulfilled demanded no less strength than heroic actions ; that you find your account in it much better, both in respect to reputation and happiness ; and that the esteem of mankind was infinitely better than sometimes their admiration.

In my opinion, idleness is no less the pest of society than solitude. Nothing contracts the mind, nothing engenders trifles, tales, backbitings, slander and falsities, so much as being shut up in a room opposite others, reduced to no other occupation than the necessity of continually chattering. When everyone is employed, they speak only when they have something to say ; but if you are doing nothing, you must absolutely talk incessantly, and this of all constraints is the most troublesome and the most dangerous. I dare go even farther, and maintain that, to render a circle truly agreable, everyone must be not only doing something, but something which requires a little attention.

When I was at Motiers, I sat down with my neighbours to make laces : should I once more mix with the world, I will carry in my pocket a cup and ball, to play with it the whole day, to dispense with talking when I have nothing to say. If everyone did so, mankind would be less wicked, their friendship more certain and I believe more agreable. In fine, let wags laugh if they will : I maintain that the only morals within the reach of the present age is the cup and ball moral.

Believers generally make God as they are themselves : good people make him good, the wicked make him mischievous ; choleric and spiteful bigots see nothing but hell, because they would be glad to damn everybody ; mild and friendly souls believe little of it, and one of the astonishments I can't get the better of is, to perceive the good Fénelon speak of it, in his *Telemachus*, as if he readily believed it : but I hope he told a lie ; for, in fact, however veridical a man may be, he must lie a little sometimes if he is a bishop. Mamma did not do so with me ; and her soul, without spleen, which could not imagine a vindictive and continually angry God, saw nothing but clemency and mercy where bigots saw nothing but justice and punishment. She often said, that there would be no justice in God in being equitable towards us ; for not having given us that which must make us so, it would be demanding more of us than He has given. The most whimsical of all was her believing in purgatory, but not in hell. This proceeded from her not knowing how to dispose of the wicked, as she could neither damn them nor place them with the good until they were become so ; it must be owned the wicked are, both in this world and the next, extremely troublesome.

When a man has a little true relish for the sciences, the first thing he finds in his pursuit is their connection, which causes them mutually to attract, assist, and enlighten each other, and that one cannot do without the other. Tho' the human mind is not sufficient to all, and must always prefer one as the principal, yet if it has not some notion of the others, it often finds itself in obscurity even with that it has chosen. I knew that what I had undertaken was good and useful in itself, and that nothing but a change of method was necessary. Beginning with the Encyclopedia, I went on, dividing it into branches ; I saw the contrary was necessary, to take (them) each one separately, and follow (them) each one by itself to the point at which they unite. Thus I came back to the ordinary synthesis ; but I came back as a man who knows what he is doing.

I was never so near wisdom as at this happy period. Without great remorse for the past, delivered from the care of futurity, the ruling sentiment of my mind was to enjoy the present. Bigots have in general a little sensuality, extremely keen, which makes them favour with delight the innocent pleasures permitted them. Worldlings impute it to them as a crime. I don't know why, or rather I do know. It is because they envy them the enjoyment of pleasures for which they have lost all taste. I had this taste, and found it pleasing to falsify it in surety of conscience. My heart as yet new gave itself into all with the pleasure of a child, or rather, if I dare say so, with the voluptuousness of an angel ; for really these tranquil enjoyments have the serenity of those of Paradise. Dinners on the grass, suppers in the arbour, gathering in the fruits, vintage, peeling flax in the evening with our people, these things were to us so many holidays. More solitary walks had still greater charms, because the mind could expand itself more freely.

I courageously renounced a sinful pleasure, with a few sighs, I own ; but also with that inward satisfaction I tasted for the first time in my life, when I could say to myself, I deserve my own esteem ; I can prefer my duty to my pleasures. This was the first real obligation I had to reading. 'Twas that which taught me to reflect and compare. After having adopted principles so pure not long before ; after those rules of wisdom and virtue I had made myself, and that I felt myself so ambitious to follow ; the shame of being so little consistent with myself, to belie so soon and so openly my own maxims, got the better of pleasure : pride had, perhaps, as great a share in my resolution as virtue, it produces effects so like it, the mistake is pardonable.

One of the advantages of good actions is to raise the soul and dispose it to better : for such is human weakness, one must add to the number of good actions an abstinence from the evil we are tempted to commit.

I thought the gospel being the same for every Christian, and the only difference in religious opinions the result of the explanations given by men to that which they did not understand, it was the exclusive right of the sovereign power in every country to fix the mode of worship, and this unintelligible dogma ; and that consequently it was the duty of a citizen to admit the one and conform to the other in the manner prescribed by the law. The conversation of the Encyclopedists, far from staggering my faith, gave it a new strength by my natural aversion to disputes and party. The study of man and the universe had everywhere shewn me the final causes and the wisdom by which they were directed. The reading of the Bible, and especially that of the New Testament, to which I had for several years past applied myself, had given me a sovereign contempt for the base and stupid interpretations given to the words of Jesus Christ by persons the least worthy of understanding his divine doctrine. In a word, philosophy, while it attached me to the essential part of religion, had detached me from the trash of the little formularies with which men had rendered it obscure. Judging that for a reasonable man there were not two ways of being a Christian, I was also of opinion that in each country everything relative to form and discipline was within the jurisdiction of the laws. From this principle so social and pacific, and which has brought upon me such cruel persecutions, it followed that, if I wished to be a citizen of Geneva, I must become a Protestant, and conform to the mode of worship established in my country.

I felt that writing for bread would soon have extinguished my genius and destroyed my talents, which were less in my pen than in my heart, and solely proceeded from an elevated and noble manner of thinking, by which alone they could be cherished and preserved. Nothing vigorous or great can come from a pen totally venal. Necessity, nay even avarice, would have made me write rather rapidly than well. If the desire of success had not led me into cabals, it might have made me endeavour to publish fewer true and useful works than those which might be pleasing to the multitude; and instead of a distinguished author, which I might possibly become, I should have been nothing more than a scribbler. No, no! I have always felt that the profession of letters was illustrious in proportion as it was less a trade. It is too difficult to think nobly when we think for a livelihood. To be able, to dare even to speak great truths, an author must be independent of success. I gave my books to the public with a certainty of having written for the general good of mankind, without giving myself the least concern about what was to follow. If the work was thrown aside, so much the worse, for such as did not choose to profit by it. Their approbation was not necessary to enable me to live; my profession was sufficient to maintain me had not my works had a sale ; for which reason, alone, they all sold.

I had perceived everything to be radically connected with politics, and that, upon whatever principles these were founded, a people would never be more than that which the nature of the government made them ; therefore the great question of the best government possible appeared to me to be reduced to this : What is the nature of the government properest to form the most virtuous and enlightened, the wisest and best people, taking the last epithet in its most extensive meaning ? I thought this question was much if not quite of the same nature with that which follows : What government is that which by its nature always maintains itself nearest to the laws ? Hence, what is the law ? and a series of questions of similar importance. I perceived these led to great truths, useful to the happiness of mankind.

It has been remarked that most men are in the course of their lives frequently unlike themselves, and seem to be transformed into others very different from what they were. It was not to establish a thing so generally known that I wished to write a book ; I had a newer and more important object. This was to search for the cause of these variations, and, by confining my observations to those which depend on ourselves, to demonstrate in what manner it might be possible to direct them, in order to render us better and more certain of our dispositions. For it is undoubtedly more painful to an honest man to resist desires already formed, and which it is his duty to subdue, than to prevent, change, or modify the same desires in their source, were he capable of tracing them to it. A man under temptation resists once because he has strength of mind, he yields another time because this is overcome; had it been the same as before he would again have triumphed.

By examining within myself, and searching in others what could be the cause of these different manners of being, I discovered that, in a great measure, they depended on the anterior impression of external objects; and that, continually modified by our senses and organs, we, without knowing it, bore in our ideas, sentiments, and even actions, the effect of these modifications. The striking and numerous observations I had collected were beyond all manner of dispute, and by their natural principles seemed proper to furnish an exterior regimen, which, varied according to circumstances, might place and support the mind in the state most favourable to virtue. From how many mistakes would reason be preserved, how many vices would be stifled in their birth, were it possible to force animal economy to favour moral order, which it so frequently disturbs! Climates, seasons, sounds, colours, light, darkness, the elements, aliments, noise, silence, motion, rest, all act on the animal machine, and consequently on the mind; all offer us a thousand means, almost certain of directing in their origin the sentiments by which we suffer ourselves to be governed.

Being past the age of romantic projects, and having been more stunned than flattered by the trumpet of fame, my only hope was that of living at ease, and constantly at leisure. This is the life of the blessed in the world to come, and for the rest of mine here below I made it my supreme happiness.

They who reproach me with so many contradictions, will not fail here to add another to the number. I have observed that the indolence of great companies made them insupportable to me, and I am now seeking solitude for the sole purpose of abandoning myself to inaction. This however is my disposition; if there be in it a contradiction, it proceeds from nature and not from me; but there is so little that it is precisely on that account that I am always consistent. The indolence of company is burdensome because it is forced. That of solitude is charming because it is free, and depends upon the will. In company I suffer cruelly by inaction because this is of necessity. I must there remain nailed to my chair, or stand upright like a picket, suffering at the same time the fatigue of inaction and all the torment of constraint; obliged to pay attention to every foolish thing uttered, and to all the idle compliments paid, and constantly to keep my mind upon the rack that I may not fail to introduce in my turn my jest or my lie. And this is called idleness! It is the labour of a galley slave.

The indolence I love is not that of a lazy fellow who sits with his arms crossed in total inaction, and thinks no more than he acts, but that of a child which is incessantly in motion doing nothing. I love to amuse myself with trifles, by beginning a hundred things, and never finishing one of them, by going and coming as I take either into my head, by changing my project at every instant, by following a fly through all its windings, in wishing to overturn a rock to see what is under it, by undertaking with ardour the work of ten years, and abandoning it without regret at the end of ten minutes; finally, in musing from morning until night without order or coherence, and in following in everything the caprice of the moment.

Botany, such as I have always considered it, and of which after my own manner I began to become passionately fond, was precisely an idle study, proper to fill up the void of my leisure, without leaving room for the delirium of imagination or the weariness of total inaction. Carelessly wandering in the woods and the country, mechanically gathering here a flower and there a branch, observing a thousand and a thousand times the same things, and always with the same interest, were to me the means of passing an eternity without a weary moment.

I know no homage more worthy of the Divinity than the silent admiration excited by the contemplation of his works. I can easily comprehend the reason why the inhabitants of great cities, who see nothing but walls, streets, and crimes, have but little faith; but not whence it happens that people in the country, and especially such as live in solitude, can possibly be without it. How comes it to pass these do not a hundred times a day elevate their minds in ecstasy to the author of the wonders which strike their senses? For my part, it is especially at rising, wearied by a want of sleep, that long habit inclines me to this elevation which imposes not the fatigue of thinking. But to this effect I must be struck with the ravishing beauties of nature. In my chamber I pray less frequently, and not so fervently; but at the view of a fine landscape I feel myself moved, but by what I am unable to tell. I have somewhere read of a wise bishop who on a visit to his diocese, found an old woman, whose only prayer consisted in the sole interjection Oh! "Good mother," said he to her, "continue to pray in this manner; your prayer is better than ours." This better prayer is mine also.